To the Cognism Marketing team,
and my husband, who now knows
more about B2B marketing than any
insurance broker should.

Contents

Introduction

I'll let you in on a secret. I love knowing what other marketing, sales or business leaders have been up to.

Maybe it's just 'cause I'm nosy...

But I like it because it's a really insightful way to learn. Either from mistakes they've made, or new ways of approaching things from trailblazers.

So I guess I'm hoping you might be the same, and that you'd be interested to learn some of the lessons I've learned through my experiences as a first-time CMO at Cognism.

Because I won't lie to you, it was intimidating at first. There were a lot of decisions resting on my shoulders, lots that could go wrong. But it's also exciting. The anticipation of all the things we could try. And how amazing it would be for them to go well.

And believe me, I've learned a lot over the last couple years. Including...

→ A CMO needs to speak multiple languages: CFO, VP Sales and CEO.
→ Marketing is a lot like playing a game of poker, your success will rely on your ability to place the right bets.
→ Execution over ideation - always.

And so I wanted to consolidate them all in one place. Introducing... (insert drum roll here)

Diary of a first-time CMO.

I know most people will tell you that you shouldn't read someone else's diary, but this can be the exception. I promise I don't mind.

I'm going to take you through my LinkedIn posts from the past two years and:

→ Tell you a bit more about what was going on during these times.
→ Why I made the decisions I did...
→ and what I've learned since.

Alright... no time like the present, let's go.

Put yourself in their shoes

 Alice De Courcy · 1st
Group Chief Marketing Officer at Cognism – Technical SaaS revenue...
3yr · 🌐

• • •

As a marketer, I don't often cold call, yesterday I did and this is what I found out:

It is very hard.

We were running a cold calling demo day and as part of the revenue team I volunteered myself and my team to join forces with sales.

Who was I calling?

I pulled up a list of contacts who had engaged with some of our content in the past few months.

Top learnings were:

1️⃣ People didn't want to:
- Speak about Cognism
- Be sold to

2️⃣ People were more receptive to:
- Talking with a marketer – it seemed to disarm them
- Giving their feedback on our content
- Talking about what they would like to read/see more of

So, how did I get on?
📱 45 dials
📞 2 follow-up calls booked in
0️⃣ demo's booked

So I don't think I will be being offered a job in sales any time soon, but the knowledge and value the team and I got from speaking to our prospects, listening to what their pain points were, their motivations for engaging with our content and what really matters to them right now was invaluable.

There is no doubt that this feedback will be far more valuable than any desk research I could have conducted.

Importantly I also have a far better understanding for what our sales team do every day and how hard it is. #salesandmarketingalignment

---

👍❤️💬 315   50 comments · 1 repost

👍 Like   💬 Comment   ↗ Share   ✈ Send

Alright, starting us off here with some behind the scenes info that provides a bit of context to this post.

At this time, we were still running e-book downloads as a huge part of our strategy, we were very much still on the MQL hamster wheel.

We had dedicated MDRs following up on content downloads and we were running extensive cold calling blitzes on a regular basis.

At this stage, our marketing team was only about 3 people and the company was maybe only 40 people in total. I was keen to drive alignment between each of the small pods, so I suggested that we join sales and made some cold calls ourselves.

We decided we'd call the content leads that we'd ordinarily send to sales. After all, we should put our money where our mouth is and see what quality we were driving. Plus, we knew we could hold our own in those conversations.

Now don't get me wrong, I certainly didn't take to it like a duck to water... but it was such a valuable experience. It was eye-opening to say the least.

Here are a few of the responses we got:

"Did I download something? I don't remember."

"Cognism... who's that? What content are you talking about?"

Or

"Oh yeah, I've got that open on my desktop but I haven't actually read it."

And they weren't terribly warm conversations either, which was a misconception we had I think.

We had expected a more friendly reception because we had thought, 'well, they've downloaded some of our content, they know who we are and must have some level of interest'.

But in reality, the reception was pretty cold. And in some cases, they may even have been more antagonistic because they didn't remember downloading the content that you're telling them they did.

So they didn't understand why you were calling, which made it nearly impossible to pitch to them afterwards.

So that was a massive learning opportunity for us, and it really was the moment that sparked that 'there must be a better way'.

We could, fortunately, still get some really valuable data from this exercise. Once we were able to get people talking.

Less about selling Cognism, but more about what our prospects cared about. What problems were they facing? What content did they find interesting?

And this really helped us shape what we did next by:

→ Learning what language they use.
→ What their views and opinions on various subjects were.
→ Getting to grips with our core personas.
→ Validating any messaging we wanted to test out.

We used this information to lead the way when creating website copy, building our messaging and positioning and ultimately putting together our content plan that allowed us to scale.

Because of the size of the marketing team at this time, I was pretty hands-on with each of these processes, so feeling like I had that insight into our prospects was super valuable.

Two key takeaways I gained from this experience are:

1. Don't be afraid of getting involved, get your hands dirty and get on the phone with your target personas.

It's really not as scary or hard as it might seem. They don't need to be customers either, prospects can give really great insights. You just need to block out time in your calendar to do it.

2. Some of the best things you can do as a CMO to move the needle, you can do for free.

For example, using the insights you've learned on the phones to rework website copy or redesign high-intent pages. These things can make a massive difference to numbers versus spending more on ads with messaging that doesn't resonate.

Honestly? I wish I'd spent more time calling prospects. It can lead to such quick wins, and costs no money.

Any first-time CMO who comes in saying I think I can improve xyz figures and do it without spending any money... just using your own time. Well, that's a massive win.

Again, I won't lie to you. When I started as a CMO, I felt like I was blagging it. So I decided I'm just going to try to be the cheapest, most hard-working CMO out there and bring the best value I can offer.

So that was my mentality. And as you can imagine, that went down well with finance, and the CEO. If you're able to make an impact without spending any-thing... of course they're going to be happy! This is one area where you can defi-nitely do that.

Test your boundaries

 Alice De Courcy · 1st
Group Chief Marketing Officer at Cognism - Technical SaaS revenue...
3yr · 🌐

I am an introverted marketer. So how do I start marketing myself better?

Over my career I have had lots of PDP meetings and one thing that always comes up: get yourself out there more.

This year I have promised myself I will keep pushing my comfort zone to do exactly that. So what have I done?

1 I started moderating the webinars I was promoting. Very daunting at first, but instead of spending the time briefing someone else to moderate you can use this time to prep yourself.

2 I took part in our company cold calling day, probably the scariest of all the things I did, but the most rewarding too. Even if your company doesn't have a cold calling day, speak to sales and see if you can spend some time calling prospects.

3 When I was asked to speak at an event, I said yes! I kept the talk to what I really knew - all the strategies I have been implementing over the past year. This made it far less daunting.

4 I am going to share the talk in the comments with you for feedback. Also pretty scary! I definitely have a lot to improve on and would love to hear your thoughts so that I can keep progressing and pushing myself. #personalbranding

👍❤️ 128   32 comments · 1 repost

👍 Like   💬 Comment   ↗ Share   ✈ Send

If you follow me now on LinkedIn or have seen any of my content online, you might think public speaking comes fairly naturally to me.

You might even think I enjoy it – that I'm an extrovert.

But that's not at all how I started.

Yes, now I'll moderate or host a webinar or speak directly to the camera without much thought, but don't be fooled, I'm an introvert.

I remember the first time I introduced using webinars at Cognism – which was an amazing quick win, they'd never done them before so it was a great opportunity.

We had plenty of in-house expertise to utilise and it would cost next to nothing to implement. However, I knew I was going to have to be the one to moderate the call.

While I'd sat outside of brilliant webinars in the past, I'd never moderated one myself. But there were no alternatives, it had to be me. So how do you bridge the gap?

I'm afraid I don't have any magic recipe to fix this problem, my only advice is to get comfortable with feeling uncomfortable. The more you practise, the better you get.

In the early days of running webinars, I was so scared. I'd have a script, and if anything, I'd say I would over-prepare.

That just meant I was stunted and awkward. I couldn't respond in a way that felt natural 'cause I was so restricted by my script.

But with experience and time, that fear started to dissipate.

Once I realised that I was able to answer questions, and that I did actually know what I was talking about, my confidence grew.

If I were to give someone in this position advice, I'd say stick to topics you're comfortable talking about – initially – while you find your feet. Because once you get going on a topic you enjoy talking about, the rest fades away.

I had a similar experience when I first started posting to LinkedIn. I thought nothing I was saying was valuable and I would have no engagement on my posts.

(A quick nod to the full circle moment here, talking about how I was scared to post to LinkedIn, now I'm sharing all my posts again and going into more detail. Funny how the world works sometimes, eh?)
Anyway, I was sitting at my desk, spending ages poring over my post, trying to make sure it was perfect. And I struggled to press share.

And of course, eventually – I did, because we wouldn't be here doing this.

But one thing I'd love to tell anyone struggling like I was is that we can all learn from one another.

You don't need to know everything right now, and the people around you can learn with you as you go.

No matter what your experience, your seniority, if you have a story to tell, there are people who will want to listen and learn from you.

I can now spend four or five minutes writing up a post, and I'll publish it without too much thought. But that didn't happen overnight. You have to commit to doing it regularly. Repetition is key.

We are in an age now where your personal brand is important. It can help propel you in your career, and it can help the businesses you work for as well.

So getting comfortable with putting yourself into the public eye is a great lesson to learn.

Lessons I've learned about marketing and sales alignment

Alice De Courcy · 1st

Group Chief Marketing Officer at Cognism - Technical SaaS revenue...

3yr · 🌐

Sales and Marketing alignment - is this just another one of those posts? ☐

I hope not.

What practical steps can you take to make this a real reality in your business?

[1] Stop referring to Sales and Marketing separately, start calling yourself a Revenue Team.

[2] Measure Marketing in the same way as Sales, at Cognism my team is measured by the same metrics as the Outbound Team.

[3] Look at hybrid roles to improve connectivity and feedback loops - we have introduced Marketing Development Rep roles - tying your success closely together will really drive alignment.

[4] Walk a day in each other shoes - the marketing team cold calls once a quarter - no better way to understand each other than by trying it for yourself.

[5] Get Sales involved in Marketing activities: employee spotlight videos, speakers on webinars, contributors to blogs etc.

[6] Over communicate. Internal comms with the Sales team are just as important as your lead generation campaigns and in the same way they need to be multi-channel, multi-touch.

This can all be achieved remotely as well and for me step 2 is fundamental to success and lasting alignment. #remoteworking #salesandmarketingalignment #workfromhome

🗨💚♡ 96   50 comments · 1 repost

👍 Like   💬 Comment   ➡ Share   ✈ Send

Okay, this might be a long one. I have some bits and bobs to add to each of my points here.

No. 1

Rewinding back to when I first started at Cognism, I was hired by the CRO at the time. She was a phenomenal leader, and she really set the tone I wanted to follow in terms of marketing and sales alignment.

She asked me to join her in a meeting with the Sales Director and UK Head of SDRs and we all decided on one key goal and one core metric. Revenue.

She also made sure to refer to us as a team. A revenue team. And with a CRO leading the way, looking after both marketing and sales, that structure lends itself well to alignment between the two teams.

Now that's no longer our set up today, but that's not really what matters. What does matter, is that we still drive towards that shared goal.

We meet consistently to have sessions where we...

→ Review our goals.

→ Work out where we are in relation to meeting these goals.

→ Decide what else we can do to reach where we want to be.

A recent example:

We've seen our lead to meetings booked conversation rate on inbounds decrease consistently for the last few months.

Our inbound reps who qualify any of our inbound demand sit within the Sales Director's team. He is also tied to the revenue goal, and he knows that over 50% of that revenue is generated by marketing.

So he knows for him to do well, these reps have to do well.

So we are all aligned that we need this 'lead to meeting booked' metric to improve in order to reach our revenue goals and ultimately positively impact the business.

And we now have a plan in place to tackle this problem.

That might sound like a small thing - however the number of people who we need buy-in from, especially at the stage of growth Cognism is at, this is huge.

This simply wouldn't be possible if we didn't have this alignment between the two departments.

I really feel it's this shared goal that allows us to really care about coming together to solve problems as a wider team.

No. 2

I feel like I've touched on some of this in lesson no.1, but something I'd like to add here is about having a shared destiny.

Our monthly revenue operations meeting is completely impartial and only focuses on the facts and figures. It's chaired by the RevOps team. And if I went in there and said: 'great, the marketing team is delivering our MQL number'.

But on the other side of the table, sales are telling us their reps aren't meeting quota. It can become a difficult discussion where teams can feel pitted against each other.

But we have found that we can use these meetings to work together to find the gap.

For example, is it because we need to hire more SDRs? Or do we need to spend more on marketing? Is there a problem with the conversation rate?

We use this time to find solutions together. And that comes back to us tying our destinies together.

No. 3

I spoke a lot about MDRs at the beginning of my role at Cognism. That's because while we were still running the MQL playbook, MDRs were the best way of optimising this.

These reps were solely responsible for qualifying the demand created by marketing. Whether that was through content downloads or other inbounds.

Through this dedicated role, we managed to make a big improvement in our conversion rate. We increased lead to meeting booked on content downloads from 5% to 15%.

So if you were going to go down this MQL route, then definitely consider having a dedicated role like this. Instead of sending inbounds to your SDRs.

This role also acts as another link into sales which helped to keep us on track and aligned. They can provide feedback on the quality of the leads (or the lack of quality). As well as what types of content converted well in conversations.

But if you don't already know, we've changed up our strategy quite a bit since then. This approach did work for us, for a time. But as we grew, it wasn't workable to scale to the level we needed.

No. 4

I'd highly recommend a quarterly session where you get your marketing team involved in cold calling. Get them into the sales team's shoes.

Find out things like:

→ Questions prospects ask.
→ The common objections they get.
→ How the process works for your sales team.

Which can help you to create a better list of resources for both your prospects and sales team to bridge the knowledge gaps.

This allows your sales team to do their jobs better and find ways in which the process in general could be improved.

And this doesn't have to just be you joining in on the cold calling. You could also:

→ Join in on a scheduled meeting or demo.
→ Listen to previous call recordings.
→ Be on the sales floor when the sales team are making calls.

No. 5

And vice versa. It would be great to get the sales team involved in the marketing organisation. Show them it's not just colouring in or pushing some buttons!

I don't mean only getting a sales rep to shadow a marketer for a day.

- We're very lucky that our sales reps are actually our ICP, so we're keen to get them involved in a lot of the content we produce.

- Because of this, they're much closer to the process, they can see the output and the time it takes to execute. As a result, they also tend to have much higher interest to see how the content performs.

- They see themselves in videos promoted on LinkedIn and the response they get from viewers who want to connect with them after.

This is a really powerful way to align these two organisations.

No. 6

Overcommunication is key, especially when you're new to an organisation.

When I joined Cognism, marketing existed solely to serve sales. Any requests they had, we would do. We weren't yet tied to a revenue target. We acted by reacting to what sales wanted from us.

So going from this state, to the state we are in today was a big jump.

We didn't want to alienate anyone by completely flipping the way of working overnight without a good explanation. I can't imagine that would have won me any popularity awards.

This was more of an iterative process over time, and each step of the way, I'd over-communicate what I was doing.

By over-communication, I mean sharing:

→ The plan you're creating.
→ The reasons behind the plan.
→ Using simple language without jargon.
→ What you're trying to achieve and how.
→ How this new plan will benefit them.
→ Continuing to communicate the results of this over time.

You can't communicate enough, especially when you're changing the way things are done. Focus just as much on your internal marketing as you do your external.

Growing a team

When I mentioned I was going to be writing this diary, one of the questions I was asked was:

'Will you talk about how you grew your team from 3 to more than 39+ people?'

And at first, I didn't really understand why people would find that interesting, but they explained:

'I wouldn't know the first thing about when to add which resources at which stages.

→ How do you decide which roles you need?

→ How do you decide which departments to build out first?

→ And how did you justify your decisions to the exec team?'

I feel like for me, growing the team felt like a very natural evolution. There were signs and signals along the way that told me when and who to add to the team.

When I joined Cognism, it was a small group. We had someone working full-time on content, a full-time designer, and a videographer (which yes, was a bit of a luxury at the time. She was initially working on a three month project, but she was so brilliant we had to keep her).

From an outsider's perspective, you might think this was a bit of an unusual set up. If you came in fresh and were building out a team, they may not be the first roles you'd hire.

But each of those team members was driven and dedicated. All we needed to do was to build out more resources around them.

The first person I knew I needed to add to this group was another all-rounder. Someone who could help me with:

→ The paid activity.

→ Look at things from a campaign perspective.

→ Understood Pardot.

→ How to measure, track and report on any marketing activity.

→ Other light operational activity.

Because at that time, I was spanning a wider range of processes than I am now. I had to be pretty hands-on initially. So I needed another body who could help me cover each of these bases.

So I hired a Campaign Marketing Manager, who filled in that gap for me.

If I were to have joined Cognism and had to build out the team from scratch and had the same number of hires, I'd hire:

→ A wordsmith or content role.

The value of having a dedicated content person is immense. The impact you can make by producing value-led content and building out a strong SEO strategy is huge. I would definitely, 100% have a wordsmith.

→ An operations/mathematical minded brain.

I have quite an operational, mathematical type brain. So between myself and the Campaign Marketing Manager I hired, we managed a lot of the role of Marketing Ops.

We only hired dedicated RevOps/Marketing Ops roles towards the end of last year because, until then, we were able to cover these processes ourselves.

If you don't have that type of brain yourself - it's good to have a person who can think this way on board.

→ A creative, hands-on, all-round marketer who is action biased.

Ideally you'd have a marketer who can wear a lot of hats. Someone who understands email, can set up a webinar workflow, can edit landing page copy, is comfortable running paid ads on LinkedIn and more. Multi-disciplined and super hands-on.

Another really important aspect of any person you hire is that they have energy.

Any marketing team is going to run more smoothly when you have people who are eager to roll up their sleeves and get to work. But especially in the early days of a business.

And what proves that each of our initial marketing team members were the right fit for Cognism? Each of them are still here three years later.

Not only that, but they each have a team of people now working under them. They've scaled as the business did.

Our Videographer is now a Video Manager and has a new hire helping her with the vast number of videos being produced.

Our wordsmith is now a Senior Content Manager and has a whole team of content writers - from SEO experts to journalistic writers.

And our designer is now a Senior Graphic Design Manager. He has his own team of designers working on all the creative briefs coming from the wider marketing team.

Plus of course my first hire, our Campaign Marketing Manager is now our VP of Marketing.

I think this just goes to show that we built things the right way to scale when we needed to.

Another reason I know we built the team the right way was because we were able to achieve the objective I was hired for within four months.

I was asked to create a marketing function that brought in 50% of the revenue target – and granted, our targets were much lower back then. But we did it. In four months! A proud moment for me and the powerhouse team. Such an amazing milestone.

This was also a crucial moment for building out the rest of the team moving forwards. Because it was when the exec team really bought into my process and put their trust in my decision-making. This made justifying my hiring choices much easier.

But where should you go from there?

It all comes down to what's working and where the positive signals are coming from. It should be obvious from your numbers where your opportunities are. Equally, it's likely pretty obvious when you're maxed out at capacity.

For example, on the content side of things, we used our single wordsmith (along with some freelancers) for quite a while. And that worked for us because we had great workflow.

But when it came to content for paid, or campaigns, we were being slowed down by the fact that we didn't have enough people to work on them.

So it was very clear to me that this was an area we needed to add to. There was so much potential, we just needed more hands on deck.

If there was one area I wish I'd added to sooner, it would be product marketing. There's so much value from someone who is living and breathing:

→ The product.
→ Your positioning and messaging.
→ Your value proposition.
→ Delivering amazing assets across the bottom of the funnel.
→ As well as having eyes on the website, optimising copy.

All these things can have a massive impact, and we didn't have this for a long time.

Unfortunately there's no secret formula for building a team. You will need to make decisions based on your gut feeling, but you can use the signals around you to lead the way.

Scaling marketing teams is more complicated than sales teams. With sales teams, if you double the people, you can likely double the revenue. But with marketing teams, it's not so linear.

At one stage, I was asked to double our budget, and double our revenue target. We still had a team of four people.

I had to come up with a method for deciding how we would scale this spend.

I realised that I needed to allocate some of this budget to hiring new heads in marketing. And not spend it all on paid. Otherwise, we would end up being inefficient and unable to scale further.

So I put in a proposal for new hires, positioning it to the other execs as the way to manage that spend correctly.

But no matter what your journey through scaling is, I think as long as you are hands-on and involved in all the processes. You'll see the gaps and you'll know where to build first.

In summary:

1. Make sure you have the core skills you need.
2. Use the data to inform where your biggest opportunities are.
3. When you reach capacity and can no longer make the best of those opportunities, fill the gaps with new hires. Look for people with energy and biassed to action.
4. Continue to review over time as your strategy, goals and skills evolve.

ENTRY 4:

Data is everything

 Alice De Courcy · 1st
Group Chief Marketing Officer at Cognism - Technical SaaS revenue...
2yr · 🌐

···

The other day I sat down with Declan Mulkeen from Strategic IC to discuss everything data and ABM.

Anyone who knows me will know that I am a big believer in the importance of data.

Data is the means by which you can engage with your customers and prospects, it's the key to personalisation, it provides you with insights, and it's the foundation for building predictable revenue from marketing.

Data underpins all aspects of your ABM campaigns, and if you can get this piece right it can give you a key differentiator against your competition, allowing you to engage with more of your target prospects and accounts.

Check out the full interview by following the link below 👇

#abm #datadrivenmarketing #b2bmarketing #b2bleadgeneration

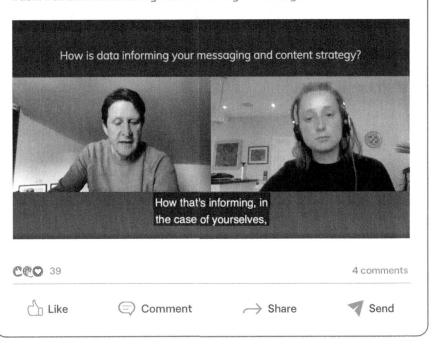

😀🥰❤️ 39   4 comments

👍 Like   💬 Comment   ↗ Share   ✈ Send

My first day at Cognism, I wanted to see all the data. Show me the data!!

But there really wasn't very much to see.

Nothing was really tracked in-platform and nothing really tracked through to the CRM. We didn't have any UTMs or a process around how to use them and no hidden fields on our forms.

So even the stuff that was working, wasn't really being tracked. So it was hard to say where to go at that point.

So my first port of call was to put in foundational tracking – an easy win.

We're going to make decisions that are both art and science. But in order to make these choices, we need a foundational understanding of our data to guide us.

So what did I do?

→ I implemented UTMs.
→ Added hidden fields onto forms.
→ I made sure Pardot and our CRM were updated with the fields needed to receive this data.
→ And applied consistency across our marketing activity so we could track our results.

It was exhilarating the first time I saw the UTMs come through on Salesforce, and I could start populating reports. It was such a small win, but so important to everything that came next.

I was able to see which of our channels were working and what content people were engaging with. It put us in a much better position to decide what to do next.

Data is the foundation of everything you want to build. Don't underestimate how crucial it is.

I think that was one thing the exec team really liked about what I brought to the table - that I measured as much as I could.

For example:

We had no way of measuring the success of the events we were holding. So I worked out a model for tracking the full cost and ROI for these events - and that ended up being very impactful.

We realised that events weren't profitable for us anymore, so we pivoted away from the event strategy. And we moved into something that would be more predictable and scalable. Without that data, we wouldn't have been able to make that decision.

Having said that, I've had to get very comfortable with the idea that I can't measure everything. Especially now we're executing a demand generation strategy. You simply cannot track every metric.

So I've learned to look for trends or correlations in data versus exact numbers and direct attribution.

The main thing is that you don't have data for data's sake. It has to have a use, there has to be some kind of commentary, analysis or discussion around it.

Without those things, data is just a busy task that sits and does nothing.

Lessons on e-books

Alice De Courcy · 1st
Group Chief Marketing Officer at Cognism - Technical SaaS revenue...
2yr · 🌐

Is the eBook dead? 💀

I had a great debate on this with Chris Walker of Refine Labs yesterday.

My take on the eBook 👇

- It should always be the output of a larger SEO, content strategy

- It should be the end result of incremental value/content deposits across a quarter

- These incremental content deposits act as your litmus test to the level of engagement you will get from your eBook (They are you MVP tests)

- If the content is quality, and the targeting is right, your follow-up isn't wasted effort

- Use specialist MDR's not SDR's to run your follow-up

- Ensure the MDR's are incentivised and measured to drive results that make your eBook ROI positive

- Get more creative with how you promote your eBook. Gif's, short video's, webinars - there is huge value there

For us, the eBook is very much alive and well, 49 deals, 50k MRR, 600k ARR, in the last 5 months 💪

To listen to the full debate check out the link 🔗 in the comments and big thanks to Chris as it's always good to challenge your own thinking and Chris had some great insights and perspectives to offer as well.

Sum of initial Contract Value: 50k

🫱💙❤️ 39   9 comments

👍 Like   💬 Comment   ➡️ Share   ✈️ Send

There's a part of me that believes anything done well can work. And we definitely got good at the e-book game.

We used subject matter experts to create genuinely valuable content. We always made sure there were loads of actionable takeaways and we led with them up-front.

We wanted to make sure that people knew the quality they would get when they signed up. We did this by minimising any trickery and showing the value off the bat.

We were able to get downloads of our e-books for about $10 which was unheard of on LinkedIn.

We also got really good at converting those leads. I've mentioned this in this diary before, but we carved out the role of the MDR.

The MDR role focused solely on converting marketing generated demand. Because their sole focus were these content leads; they were great at getting them over the line.

Plus the feedback loop between them, our prospects and then back to us, was super-valuable. We knew which content resonated and which didn't. We started to understand what assets made conversations and pitching easier for our MDR's and which didn't.

We took our conversion rate from lead to SQO from 5% to 15%.

So that was really what helped to make this model so predictable and effective for us.

However there are limitations... we did get to a point of diminishing returns.

Yes, we had this predictable engine where we were generating:

→ MQLs for $10 each.
→ Converting at a rate of 15% from content lead to SQO.
→ Those would close at a rate of 12%.
→ And we knew that 1 MDR needed 400 MQLs a month to keep them at capacity.

This gave us a really simple model; it was easy to demonstrate to finance what our spend might look like from content and the revenue we could expect.

But we ran into a problem...

It only worked for the certain stage of growth we were at. Once we became more aggressive, this model was no longer viable.

Another problem we ran into was more of a team/people issue:

Salespeople get a lot of kudos/gratification from booking a meeting from a cold call. But for whatever reason, there's a perception that a lead coming from a content download was an 'easier sell'.

As we know from my first diary entry, that is certainly not the case.

However, that was the perception and so somehow there was less satisfaction coming from those deals.

One way we got around this was to make the MDR role a promotion from SDR before becoming an AE. Not only did it help the branding of the role, it also lent itself well as part of the experience and training in the sales team's progression.

But as we came to terms with the fact that we were no longer getting the same results as we scaled, it became clear I needed to rethink this process as part of our overall strategy.

I still hold the belief that if we were at that same stage in growth as before, we could still be successful using this method. As I said at the beginning of this entry, anything done well can work.

However, I do feel like today's buyers are no longer interested in downloading an e-book.

That's not how they want to engage with content anymore. They don't want to give up their details for a 20-page PDF, and I believe there are better ways to engage with your audience.

Personally, if I were starting day one at Cognism all over again... I wouldn't roll out the e-book play.

I would go with the demand generation approach that we have now.

That being said, I think if you applied all the learnings that we did back then, there's no reason you couldn't still find success using it, if you felt it had to be a part of your overall strategy.

I know it sounds like I'm very evangelical about demand generation, and I am - now. But I wasn't always.

It's kinda a funny story...

I'm sure you'll have heard of Chris Walker, if you've looked into demand generation before. He's extremely passionate about it. He was all over LinkedIn being... let's say, negative, about the e-book.

At this time, I was still finding a lot of success with the e-book model. So I felt a little defensive. I thought I'd go head-to-head with him and debate it out.

I got him onto the Cognism podcast, where we discussed the e-book and its place in the marketing function. We had a really interesting conversation.

But I remember he said to me:

'I want to do this again in a year's time, and you tell me where you are then.'

I was pretty adamant that I wouldn't change my mind. But after seeing the scalability issues with our method, and being exposed to more of his content...

Well, I did start to change my mind. He was right after all.

And we did redo the podcast - by then, we had become customers of Refine Labs. We were fully bought into the demand generation approach.

I think it's a funny to reflect on how all this stemmed from Chris Walker's posts on LinkedIn, and how my opinions changed over time.

Advice to any other first-time CMOs out there, don't let a philosophical viewpoint or an 'I've always done this' mindset prevent you from trying things a new way. I could not have been a bigger advocate of lead generation when I started my journey, and now I am known for my demand generation content and both have enabled me to scale the Cognism marketing machine to where it is today. Both have had a critical role to play.

Quality over quantity

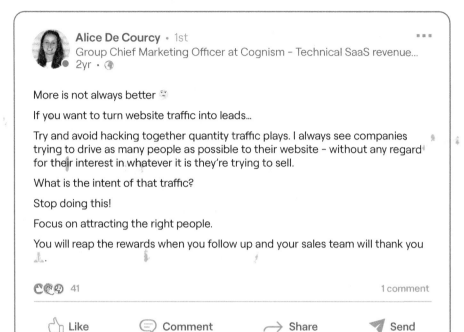

Alice De Courcy · 1st

Group Chief Marketing Officer at Cognism – Technical SaaS revenue...

2yr · 🌐

More is not always better 😬

If you want to turn website traffic into leads...

Try and avoid hacking together quantity traffic plays. I always see companies trying to drive as many people as possible to their website – without any regard for their interest in whatever it is they're trying to sell.

What is the intent of that traffic?

Stop doing this!

Focus on attracting the right people.

You will reap the rewards when you follow up and your sales team will thank you 🙏.

41   1 comment

👍 Like   💬 Comment   ➡ Share   ✈ Send

Sometimes, it's not always the best decision to do what your competition is doing. Of course, the opposite can also be true - you can learn from your competition.

But there was a tactic that most of our competitors were using that I was getting a lot of internal pressure to implement at Cognism. But I just didn't feel it aligned with our goals.

What was this tactic?

Well, essentially they'd index their databases and get SEO rankings for pages that showcased their contact and company data. Meaning they'd have individual profile pages generated online via their data engine.

It meant they had thousands of visitors per month, and lots of SEO rankings.

But I never pursued that project. Why?

Because every time I took a deep dive into the traffic health and value, I couldn't align the data with our Cognism strategy. I mean, we're talking about their top ranking being for McDonald's phone number or something similar.

And that doesn't align with what I consider Cognism to be. We're a premium sales intelligence solution, with premium data. Compliance and quality are our core values. That's what we are about.

I didn't feel that tactic would ever result in traffic that would be serious about buying Cognism.

Remember, we also had limited resources at this point. We had one content writer. I didn't want to waste time on a tactic that wasn't laser focused on building quality high intent demand.

The most important being ranking for high commercial intent keywords. The type of keywords where we know they're in the market for a product like Cognism when they search. These people have a far higher likelihood of being a better fit for us.

And that tactic and approach has paid off for us. We've seen $250,000 value in traffic that comes to our website organically which is a massive win. We also don't get as much of the junk to filter out, which means we have great conversion rates.

And that stems from focusing on quality, not quantity.

Going back to the competitors' tactic and my decision to drop it...
It wasn't an easy decision to make when there was so much pressure to give it a go. But I really believed it wasn't the right move, so I backed myself and I'm glad I did.

Interested in some quick wins for high intent, quality traffic? Here's a few things I've learned:

→ Make sure you cover your bases with your competitors. For example, SEO ranking pages detailing you versus your competitors. Plus your competitor vs another competitor. People searching for that kind of information are likely in the market to buy right now and are evaluating their options.

→ Do your research. Find every possible keyword you can rank for and bucket them into the top, middle, and bottom of the funnel. What's their ease for ranking? What do you believe their commercial intent is? Remember, some of this is more of an art than a science.

→ Analyse your Google Ads. What are the keywords that are driving conversions here? More importantly, conversions that result in revenue. For example, for us, terms like 'B2B contact data', or 'top B2B contact provider' are key revenue generating terms.

→ Use this information to inform which keywords you want to target for organic traffic.

→ Track the success of each of your pages. Which are driving the most demo requests? This helps you to decide which pages to focus on building out, and updating. And which don't have the high intent traffic you initially thought.

Value customer loyalty

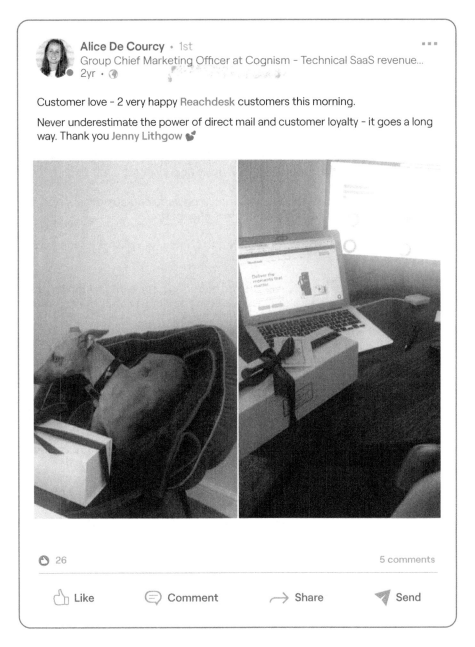

If you spend a lot of money on a gorgeous exotic plant, but then don't take the time to give it water and sunlight, it won't last very long.

Not a great investment... I'm sure we can all agree.

But if you do provide it with the light and nutrients it needs to thrive, it grows and looks beautiful for years to come.

In a roundabout way, that's why customer marketing is so important.

It's about continuing to educate, excite and nurture the people who have invested in your business, so they want to stick around – and hopefully expand and renew.

You can see that customer marketing is growing in popularity in the B2B SaaS world. But it's something I think is still massively undervalued.

I've been guilty of this too – focusing too much on acquiring customers. And not enough time keeping our current customers engaged.

But it's important to keep this process alive, to continue to give consistent value all of the time.

We put so much time, money and effort into nurturing people into becoming customers. It seems such a waste to throw it all out the window after they commit.

Because our job isn't done.

If you do customer marketing well, you then have a powerhouse brand with hundreds or thousands of brand advocates. They can then feed into the content you put out on the demand generation side.

If you think I'm wrong about how many companies do customer marketing. Do a quick search on LinkedIn to see how many people have dedicated customer marketing roles. It's not that many. And it's nowhere close to the number of demand gen roles.

We hired a Global Head of Customer Marketing and a Senior Customer Marketing Exec. They work together to enable our customers. While also ensuring our demand generation messaging reaches them.

This post on LinkedIn was a simple appreciation post. Sharing for the positive experience and treatment I had at Reachdesk (who we're still a customer of today).

Customer marketing is still a relatively new and emerging focus area within marketing. So there's no set blueprint for how it's done right now and we're still finding our feet at Cognism.

But we've split it out into four main categories:

- → Advocacy.
- → Expansion.
- → Retention.
- → Community.

And within each of those categories there is a whole variety of activities that can be done.

Of those four, I believe that retention is one of the most important levers you can pull. Especially in a B2B SaaS company where you want to scale your growth.

Acquiring new customers is expensive. So it's unrealistic to be growing at an optimal rate if you're losing customers through a leaky bucket on the back end.

Retaining them, increasing their LTV and ultimately making your money back from the cost of acquiring them is going to be a lot more successful.

So we want to put as much effort into our customer marketing as we do on our demand generation. That means investing in it accordingly moving forwards.

CMO of a startup

When you envision a marketing career, you might think becoming a Head of Marketing is where that journey ends, but that just isn't true.

Even when you become a CMO, it doesn't end. Because then you can become a Global CMO, or if you acquire multiple businesses, then you become a CMO of multiple business units.

It's a continuously evolving role that has the potential to expand. I had never thought about that before becoming one myself.

So a piece of advice I'd give to any aspiring or first-time marketing leader is to put yourself in the best position for opportunities.

For example:

There's always the chance that a company will hire above you when marketing requirements expand. But you can limit that chance by doing everything in your power to do the best you can in the role you're in today, and thinking about how that role could evolve moving forwards.

That was a big lesson for me, and luckily I had the benefit of watching some of my mentors go through this process ahead of me - so I had an idea of what to expect.

I could learn from them, prepare myself and think about the opportunities before they presented themselves. And ultimately I put myself in a strong position when the company required a global CMO, and a CMO spanning multiple business units.

The key difference in this for me was developing an ability to strategise:

- What's the Cognism marketing strategy?
- How does this change when we acquire a new brand, how do they come together or not come together?
- What are the road rules, how do we scale these two brands together or separately?
- Then present these ideas and strategies to the CEO and the board. Do it in a way that showcases you've covered all of your bases and you're capable to think outside of your current remit.

As of a few months ago, Cognism and Mailtastic added a third brand into the group mix - Kaspr. Which is all very exciting, and I'm sure I'll get a little more into that later on in this diary.

Taking things back a little first:

To when Cognism first 'met' Mailtastic, and how that acquisition all came about.

(Insert twinkling storytelling music here...)

Once upon a time, in my early days at Cognism, James (CEO) asked me to find him an email signature management tool.

I didn't have a lot of budget, so I went out and did my due diligence, researching the market to find what we needed.

Mailtastic was a German company, it was relatively young and hadn't yet really started translating into English, but they had a brilliant product. In my opinion, it was years ahead of some of its competition but for a fraction of the price - so it was an easy choice.

And we were super-happy with our experience using it once we'd been onboarded. It was really easy to use and did everything we needed it to.

So when it came to discussing possible acquisitions, James already knew we were happy customers. It fit into the marketing side of our product offering and it felt like it made a lot of sense as an acquisition play.

So Mailtastic became part of the Cognism family, and that was my first chance at stepping into that CMO role at such a strategic level.

I had to:

→ Decide whether we would integrate the brands or keep them separate.

→ Build a whole go-to-market function for Mailtastic (which was a very interesting part of the journey)

→ All at the same time as continuing to scale Cognism (because the targets there don't stop either!)

But that's what I've loved about this role. Rapid growth, constant new challenges and opportunities, plus I'm learning new things all of the time.

And I feel very grateful for the opportunity to do this. We're very lucky to have an amazing CEO who:

1. Understands marketing and is willing to invest in it.
2. Willing to invest in talent internally before looking externally.

If he can see you working hard, believes you have potential and you have a track record of getting results, then you will get invested in.

There's no end to that journey either, and I suppose I'm living proof of that. I feel you can see that throughout the marketing team, in the sales org and throughout the whole company.

For example, some people might feel like the people at Cognism are quite young for the roles they hold. But actually that's the unique vision from our CEO.

He wanted to build a team with a lot of energy.

I believe it's beneficial to give people who have never done a role like this before a chance. Because as long as they have the skills and willingness to do it, they'll work harder to prove that they can.

Also... just because you've held that role before, doesn't mean you'll be good at it. Experience doesn't always = better.

Anyway, back to my LinkedIn post.

We won a place on this list in 2020, and 2021.
This is huge kudos to the marketing team. And it shows how we've gone about building a brand and sharing what it's like working at Cognism.

Meaning it's not just about how we look to our prospects, but also how we're perceived as an employer. How we foster our talent and how that talent grows.

So getting a mention in LinkedIn's Top Startups List is great recognition for all the hard work we put in! Especially as when we were first named on that list, we were much smaller than the majority of the other brands.

We were definitely punching above our weight. I think we were making the right bets and starting to get noticed. Even at this early stage of my tenure as CMO.

Day 1 as a marketing leader

 Alice De Courcy · 1st

Group Chief Marketing Officer at Cognism – Technical SaaS revenue...

3yr · 🌐   • • •

Day 1 in your first role as a marketing leader – where do you start? 😅

Caveat – assuming you have got to know the team, key stakeholders, understood the business goals and spent time speaking to customers – so what's next?–

You've updated your email signature and LinkedIn to ⚡ Head of Marketing ⚡🍾 Let's not deny it – we all get excited about this bit – it's what you've worked so hard for.

Ok now the tough bit – how not to get fired!?

✅ Get access to the metrics 📈

What's being tracked, how is it being tracked and what does the picture look like?

✅ Get any missing tracking in place 📊

Any day or time lost on data is precious, it's your key to building the strategy and understanding what needs to be done

✅ Get started 🐌

Hit the ground running with your best growth experiment. Hit or miss, it'll get the ball rolling!

✅ Cup of tea ☕

Okay, maybe start with this one. More to come! Up next – what to kill.

#growthmarketing

☕💬👍 67   4 comments

👍 Like   💬 Comment   ➡ Share   ✈ Send

Did I worry about getting fired in the early stages?

Yeah, every day. Even now, I still have a fear of getting fired. That's something that sits in my stomach every day. But especially in the early days.

Thing is, I knew I could offer energy, relentless hard work and ideas that I could execute. Which I hoped would at least help me become one of the cheapest, most operational CMOs out there, and that had to hold some value.

That was the mentality I had. Just continue to work hard, continue to execute, as long as you continue to add value then you're going to be okay. That value is going to compound over time and it will drive impact incrementally.

So initially, I wasn't the high-level strategic thinker that I evolved into. I was definitely more hands-on and operational. Trying to execute as much as I could, and that was the mindset I tried to instil in my team as well.

I think if you're action biassed then things tend to fall in your favour.

When I reflect on my plans when I joined Cognism, I think I had set out some steps for myself, like:

→ Look under the hood, what's working and what's not?
→ Understand our personas (specifically the sales persona that I knew much less about)
→ Start building out some short term plans - what was going to have the biggest and fastest impact with minimal investment?

I didn't want to have to go to the CFO asking for £20,000 to do xyz because I didn't think that would go down well.

But I was also starting to look at the long-term plays too.

I think it's really easy to get lost in the easy short-term wins, but if you want to have any chance of scaling, you need long-term compounding plans. You need to do both.

Because I was doing a lot of the hands-on day-to-day work, like setting ads live, creating landing pages, building reports and UTM infrastructure. I found it much easier to find the long and short-term wins because I could see them. I was involved in everything.

Now something I need to be super-honest about... I don't have some secret time machine that meant I could be across all things everywhere, while also making the plans for what's next.
This time had to come from somewhere, and it often spilled into my evenings and weekends. I don't want to pretend that there's some easy other way for this to be done.

It was a lot of grind, and a lot of it was in my own time. For example, I once took two days annual leave just to focus on strategy. I needed out of the day-to-day work, so I 'took some time off'.

My fear was that if I only focused on strategy and didn't deliver on the day-to-day stuff in my first month. That wouldn't have been acceptable.

I had evaluated in my head, 'what's the worst outcome?'

I felt I'd be happier if I got feedback telling me to be less hands-on, and be more strategic after being in the role for a month. Instead of getting the question 'what have you actually achieved this month?'. And having nothing to show.

I still hold that philosophy today. If someone asks me what I've done in the week, I want to be able to list off exactly what I've managed to execute. I can show them what I've delivered, plus the outcomes of that. Not just fluffy high-level strategic plays.

And to this day, my most common bit of feedback from the CEO is 'allow yourself to be more strategic. You can be less operational.' And I've worked on that gradually. But I still believe the value of my role often still sits in the operational side of things.

At the time when I wrote this post on LinkedIn, I was trying to share that there are more ways to be a CMO. And I wish I'd had a resource that taught me how to get started as a marketing leader.

So I suppose I was trying to share my learnings with other potential aspiring future leaders. The glamorous bits, and the not-so-glamorous bits...

Some people may think being a CMO just means being in lots of meetings and making a couple of decks. But it isn't, and that's especially true in an early-stage organisation.

You don't start out with a big team full of resources and budgets to chuck around. You have to start scrappy and make growth materialise.

You need to have an idea that could move the needle. You need to be able to create an actionable plan for how you'll get there, and actually be able to follow through on it.

A creative CMO who has amazing ideas is only useful if they can make their plan come to fruition. Because if you can't then ultimately you're not making any impact.

It's an underrated skill to be able to see an amazing idea out in the world, and be able to operationalise it into your business. Taking the parts that fit your organisation, and adapting the bits that don't. We can all share a great idea or example on a slack channel. But it takes a certain type of person to deliver that back in value to your organisation by executing it.

Cut the BS

 Alice De Courcy · 1st
Group Chief Marketing Officer at Cognism - Technical SaaS revenue...
1yr · 🌐   ...

✅ Step 2 in your first marketing leadership role

You managed not to get fired in weeks 1&2😏.

Now it's time to start removing those things that don't work.

WHAT TO KILL:

☠️ The Faceless Blog

Your content strategy needs an overhaul. Is your blog just for show? Is there a strategy behind it or are marketing just being told what to write by other parts of the business? Start creating content that converts.

✖️ The Formal Tone

B2B doesn't have to mean boring! Don't forget that *real people* read your emails / posts / dream journal.

📖 Marketing as Sales Enablement

Does Marketing's position in the business need changing? Take on a revenue target, own it, and then take back control of the function. You are there to hit your number, not solely to serve the rest of the business units. Note – you can't do the latter without doing the former.

#growthmarketing

👏👍❤️ 74   7 comments

👍 Like   💬 Comment   ➡️ Share   ✈️ Send

Firstly, I'd like to reiterate that I'm in the fortunate position where the CEO believes and trusts in marketing.

This was definitely a factor in me being able to change the status quo and the 'we've always done things this way' kind of attitude. I was able to present ideas for new ways of doing things, and cull some of the old things I didn't believe were worth our time.

For example, with our content strategy.

We're in a competitive market, there's so much sales and marketing content out there. But content can be a competitive advantage if it's done well.

I noticed that a lot of sales and marketing content out there in the market could be better. And I believe that's changed a little over the last year. With lots of companies focusing more on the quality of their content as they move away from lead gen tactics.

But I saw an opportunity for Cognism to make an impact and raise the bar. To make our brand known as a source of practical and actionable, forward-thinking sales and marketing content.

This was a low financial investment bet and a long term approach. If it worked, then it would continue to scale in a compounding way.

It was more recently that I developed the idea of having dedicated story finders and journalists within the content team. Separating the SEO writers from the storytellers.

This idea was born out of my desire to build Cognism into a media machine; this was something marketers were talking about doing - but no one shared how to do it. This was just the way I came up with.

It became apparent that our current writers couldn't really produce the 'story finder' type content, because they had to write for Google. They have keywords they have to go after. These dictate the kind of content they cover to match the search intent behind those keywords.

Which meant they were restricted when it came to producing stories that would resonate with our audience today.

That's not to say that the SEO stuff was bad. That's also very necessary. But it became obvious that we needed to expand the content team to include both types of writers. They're two very different things with different objectives. Our journalists help create demand for Cognism, while our SEO'ers capture the demand that already exists.

Another philosophy I wanted our writers to live by was that each piece of content should allow our readers to take away something actionable. That can make them better at their jobs. That should always be our benchmark for any content that we publish. That's what I mean when I say 'I don't want a faceless blog'. I want people to find our content through whichever channel they discover us, and instantly see the value.

By having two halves to this media machine, our journalists are freed from Google. They can publish value-led content that drives our brand forwards and delivers a competitive advantage.

We've started to see this approach pay off too, which is amazing to see.

Because there's been a wave of dark social murmurings happening around Cognism.

We can see it in the numbers, but we can also feel it. LinkedIn posts talking about content we produce, experts in the field reviewing and praising our content strategy. And lots of people sharing how they've experienced value from Cognism content.

It's something as a team that we're incredibly proud of, and we want to continue building. A brand where we are the port of call for any questions or learning around sales and marketing.

As an example, I looked at our blog traffic value side-by-side with ZoomInfo. If you compare the size of the teams and resources, they're about 20x. And yet our blog traffic value is higher (true at the time of writing).

Which simply goes to show we're talking about the right things. We're focused on the right types of content and we're delivering a lot of value.

Not only that, but every Google update has benefitted Cognism. I believe that's because we're doing content the right way, with integrity. This trend will only continue.

One other thing I'd like to touch on around the subject of content is tone.

B2B marketing tends to be very strict, rigid and boring. Writers seem to be afraid to put in anything entertaining in case they're viewed as unprofessional. But I believe that's the wrong approach.

We had a similar vibe and tone back in the day. But I wanted us to be human, more personable and less corporate, friendly and transparent.
Ultimately, I wanted our content to be content that people wanted to read.

No BS, just real-life learnings from the front line. And that's echoed in the way we work, the way we speak, in the organisational culture in general.

Again, that's something we've had to work on developing. It wasn't this way in the beginning. But step by step, we've made our tone of voice a lot more approachable, conversational and easy to consume.

Implementing a winning content strategy

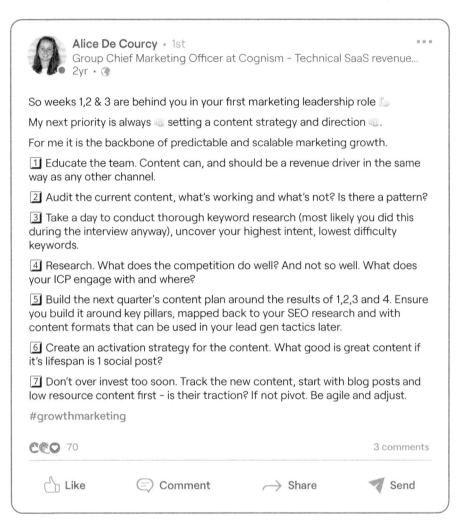

Alice De Courcy · 1st

Group Chief Marketing Officer at Cognism - Technical SaaS revenue...

2yr · 🌐

So weeks 1,2 & 3 are behind you in your first marketing leadership role 🫰

My next priority is always 👊 setting a content strategy and direction 👊.

For me it is the backbone of predictable and scalable marketing growth.

1 Educate the team. Content can, and should be a revenue driver in the same way as any other channel.

2 Audit the current content, what's working and what's not? Is there a pattern?

3 Take a day to conduct thorough keyword research (most likely you did this during the interview anyway), uncover your highest intent, lowest difficulty keywords.

4 Research. What does the competition do well? And not so well. What does your ICP engage with and where?

5 Build the next quarter's content plan around the results of 1,2,3 and 4. Ensure you build it around key pillars, mapped back to your SEO research and with content formats that can be used in your lead gen tactics later.

6 Create an activation strategy for the content. What good is great content if it's lifespan is 1 social post?

7 Don't over invest too soon. Track the new content, start with blog posts and low resource content first - is their traction? If not pivot. Be agile and adjust.

#growthmarketing

👍❤️ 70   3 comments

👍 Like   💬 Comment   ➡️ Share   ✈️ Send

I've talked a fair bit about content so far in this diary. But it's because it can be such an important lever without having to spend huge amounts of money.

Content is something I know and understand. So as a new CMO who wants to make the biggest impact with the smallest costs. I knew I could build something long-lasting if I could invest a little of my own time to refine the process.

Content is something you can track - for the most part anyway. And you can use the data available to you to deliver high value. For example, targeting high-intent keywords for SEO.

I really recommend anyone who's a new CMO to get involved in this process. Because it teaches you so much about who you're targeting. This helps to inform all your other decision-making.

Getting down and dirty in the content strategy gave me the insights I needed as a CMO to understand our buyer personas. For example, at Cognism our buyer personas are the sales persona or the marketing persona.

As a marketer myself, I felt like I knew the marketing persona. Although you should still always do your research. Don't assume you know your audience without evidence! That's a recipe for creating content that doesn't resonate.

But I didn't really know anything about the sales persona. I needed to learn what made them tick before I could do any of the work of marketing to them.

Developing the content strategy gave me the time to delve into the data around the content they engaged with. And to find the messaging that resonated. This was hugely valuable.

I needed to get into this level of insight and detail to really be confident in my plan moving forwards.

I learned that we had a good process in place where our SDRs would reach out to people who had downloaded e-books.

But, how these e-books were ideated, written, published and promoted all needed finessing.

I felt the old process was simply marketing working as a sales function. Without having the autonomy to make bold moves as a revenue-generating team in its own right.

So I decided to focus on levelling up our content. Making it more expert-led, value-led, practical and tactical.

I also overhauled our process for how we go about creating new material, such as:

→ How we decide what to work on next.

→ What we included in the content.

→ What tone of voice we used.

→ What topics we covered.

→ How we promoted it after it was finished.

I wanted us to be a brain. Using the clues around us to make smart decisions that could drive our marketing function, rather than blindly doing what we were asked to do by sales.

It all started with a deep understanding of our buyer personas. Then we would map out content based on intent and its purpose. For example:

→ Was it a piece for SEO?

→ If so, was it a pillar page?

If it was then x, y, and z would need to happen.

If the content was for an e-book for a lead gen campaign, then that sparks another series of activities.

And again, if we were creating a content piece for the blog.

We built out a clear process around each type of content, including:

→ Goals and objectives depending on the individual use case.

→ An understanding of what it would mean for each to be successful.

We used a content calendar in the early days too. We were a small team. It helped us to structure and keep track of our workflow. Especially when we needed to get work off the ground quickly.

Now that we have a larger team and dedicated content roles based on purpose, we don't. So we can be more reactive, but it's something I recommend if you're in a similar position to how we were then.

Because we were a small team with very few content roles in-house, I wanted to find ways to repurpose content to scale.

Rather than spend six weeks writing an e-book only to publish it and find out it's a flop. I would use insights from blog articles we had written in the past.

I was looking for any trends in the data and which topics we'd get the most engagement on.

We'd then use those insights to build out long-form content, compiled from relevant blog posts around a similar topic.

This meant we could still get the SEO and organic gains, while building out longer-form content that drove the lead gen plays. It meant we weren't having to reinvent the wheel each time.

Meaning we could scale fast, despite having a small team.

Any (first-time) CMO will need to plan for the resources they have. You can be clever, re-package and re-purpose, re-design and re-share. It just takes a little more planning.

For a cornerstone topic - one that we'd established had good commercial intent and interest - we would activate the content in several ways:

→ Blog articles.
→ Video/s.
→ Template/s.
→ Cadences for the sales team.
→ Email signatures.
→ Webinar/s.
→ Paid ads.
→ Organic social posts.

As I've said many times before, our budget was small, so we didn't spend a lot on content in the early days. But we did slowly learn where to invest more time, effort and money based on where we saw results or gaps.

Our focus was on quality and not quantity. So at first we invested in subject matter expertise. Instead of just hiring more writers or freelancers.

Today we have content expertise sitting in three unique areas. Each of which has proven to be vital to our scaling and stacking growth success.

1. SEO

We have two SEO experts who are 100% dedicated to working on our key SEO projects, along with maintenance and defence of our current rankings.

2. Journalists

We have two writers who are our 'story finders'. They spend time hanging out where our buyers hang out, in communities, in Slack groups, talking and listening to subject matter experts.

They're tasked with finding what's trending and writing about it in the most actionable, helpful way. Our journalists are a crucial part of our media machine approach.

3. Demand generation content executives

These are content execs who sit in a pod with DG marketers. We have two pods, each focused on a specific persona (sales or marketing).

Their responsibilities are:

→ Becoming experts in their persona.
→ Working with subject matter experts.
→ Producing content in all formats that can span and fill all four of our paid social 'create demand' buckets: Thought Leadership, Content, Product and Social Proof.
→ Briefing in scripts for videos, writing campaign-focused blog posts, or helping out with landing page copy.

As you scale, you have to think about stacking growth almost like a game of poker.

Where are you going to place your bets? How do you balance long and short-term gains?

My big bet coming into Cognism was to publish quality, expert-led content. As well as being process-driven to ensure delivery and output.

From there it's been a case of intuitively scaling this engine.

We've left behind gated content. Where we could trace the source of a deal back to a downloadable content asset. Now we run a fully ungated content model. Where we wed the content to almost every play we run.

Experiment, experiment, experiment

 Alice De Courcy · 1st
Group Chief Marketing Officer at Cognism - Technical SaaS revenue...
2yr · 🌐

Performance marketing not *performing*? Let's get testing 💀🗡

When I started at Cognism, one priority was to get paid experiments underway. Previously we had poured money into Google Ads - with no tracking in place and poor results. On day 1 I stopped all Google spend.

There was understandably a tide of nervousness around paid spend which needed to be overcome.

The key here was to run small, low budget experiments, prove the value and ramp spend gradually. You need to earn the trust to spend more. Start small.

In the first month, we overhauled all of our ads with fresh ideas. Out with the old, in with the new!

1) Start with one channel. We chose Google Ads.

2) Create a clear experiments framework to follow.

2) Follow the data-led path.

3) Don't stop there! Keep monitoring, reviewing, and iterating on your paid ads - it's not a set and forget game.

#growthmarketing

 48

👍 Like   💬 Comment   ➔ Share   ✈ Send

When I joined Cognism, our paid ads were a little all over the place...

For example:

→ All Google Ad spend had been paused, due to a previous overspend.
→ No tracking was in place.
→ Up until this point, ads had performed badly.

Now this might all sound like bad news, a bleak way to come into my new role, but I saw this as an opportunity.

This was a great example of where I could roll up my sleeves and make an impact straight away. I started by:

1. Getting our tracking in place.
2. Auditing the ad campaigns we had running and identifying the following issues:
a. Very broad keyword targeting.
b. Poor account structure, prioritisation and personalisation.

I first focused on launching just two key campaigns:

1. Brand.
2. Competitors.

As the only resource working on this project, I wanted to keep the account tight by:

→ Maximising for high intent.
→ Doubling down on changes to messaging on the landing pages to improve quality.
→ Robust tracking and data hygiene.
→ Producing ad copy that would convert.

Due to bad past experiences at Cognism (before my time), all faith had been lost in Google Ads as a channel.

So it was a very quick win to see that after only a few hours of launching my revised campaigns, we could see leads converting and being attributed correctly in Salesforce.

Later that month these leads were starting to appear on our deals whiteboard in the office, correctly attributed to Google Ads. A big win.

That was the proof I needed to show leadership that things were being properly managed. They could put their faith back in Google Ads!

It proved that Google Ads had a rightful place in our strategy.

My advice when it comes to scaling Google Ads with limited resources is to manage things closely.

You can't just set it and forget it.

You also shouldn't hand responsibility over to a cheap agency either.

Especially if they don't have access to your CRM or request access. Otherwise how can they optimise the spend for revenue? Leaving you with suboptimal optimisations and inefficiencies coming out your ears.

There are so many philosophies out there on how to run Google Ads. But it's actually as simple as keeping the account as watertight as possible.

For example, don't run more than you have the resources to manage.

Focus on the highest intent, lowest-hanging fruit first, e.g. brand and competitors.

And from there you can expand out to the highest intent, transactional keywords. Always bearing in mind your resource limitations.

It's another good idea to be running mini-experiments through your ads too. Such as checking what language your audience responds to and optimising landing page copy accordingly.

Some other experiments I ran were:

→ Including navigation on landing pages.
→ Creating multiple landing page variations to test specific messaging.
→ Gradual keyword expansion.

These changes may sound simple, but they're often overlooked. There can be some big wins in the simple things.

And we got some big wins!

→ We were getting CPLs well under our break even CPL.
→ Getting far better quality leads (that were actually converting into customers at speed!).

After Google Ads, I turned to email. But that's a whole other story in itself, so I will save that for a little later on...

The first 100 days

Alice De Courcy · 1st

Group Chief Marketing Officer at Cognism - Technical SaaS revenue...

2yr · 🌐

· · ·

How do you take on your first leadership role in marketing?

What do you need to do in your first 100 days?

I've shared my experience and some very practical tactics and processes I put in place to build a predictable marketing engine that contributes over 50% of the revenue target every month.

The first 100 days: what I learned as a new Head of Marketing

Alice de Courcy on LinkedIn · 8 min read

This article is part of a series where I will be sharing all my learnings and insights on my...

 83

12 comments · 3 reposts

 Like   Comment   Share   Send

The first 100 days are going to be when most eyes are on you.

If there is ever a time to be getting your head down and working all the hours (sorry but this is the unpopular reality), then this is it.

You need to balance immediate wins with laying down the foundations for longer term growth.

Something that helped me was having one very clear goal that I was set by the CEO and executives. To build a repeatable marketing revenue engine.

So I approached it like I would any engine repair job. I needed to work out what parts were working, what wasn't, and what was causing the most damage.

I highlighted one issue early on. The view of the engine was partially blocked by a lack of data.

So operational set-up and reporting got added to my list of 'jobs to do', but it did not block progress.

When I joined Cognism, Google Ads were shut off and Pardot was a no-go zone.

This wasn't because there was no demand for Cognism to capture via Google Ads. Or because there was no use for Pardot, but both had been poorly used before and so had been cast aside.

The caution around Google Ads was actually linked to both misuse, but also lack of reporting. I identified this as a quick win area for me to be able to clean up, optimise and start to regain trust.

I was able to get things live by focusing on the following. Brand and competitor campaigns, coupled with dedicated landing pages and forms paired with UTM tracking. And within a few hours we had leads from big brands entering our CRM and getting the correct attribution.

I could have spent weeks on a planned restructure of the account. I could have built a roadmap for campaign creation and execution. (Which I could have handed off to an agency to execute at vast expense.) But instead, I focused on grabbing the low-hanging fruit. Building trust early in order to secure buy-in longer term for wider sweeping changes.

Next up I wanted to get under the hood of the role of content at Cognism. It became clear that content was being dictated to Marketing via Sales. And it was not welded in any wider strategy or planning. The long-term play was to build out the plan and to deliver a competitive advantage through content for Cognism. But, I wanted to spend more time understanding our customers and diving into the data in order to do a good job.

So I decided in my first month that I would run a Cognism first. I would host a webinar, using external and internal speakers. And we would use Pardot to run the email campaign side of this.

Cue mass panic!

The last time Pardot had been used for mass emailing, the marketer in charge had managed to kill a number of live opps (according to Sales!) by sending the wrong email to everyone in the CRM.

The win here happened because it was a controlled activity to a focused list. It also happened through introducing a new content format to the business and showing them the value that marketing can bring to content when given ownership. So much so that after the webinar, the CEO and CRO wanted a plan for a webinar a week!

I think the point that I am trying to make is that in the first 100 days at Cognism, my goal was to build a predictable revenue model. I could have got lost in the building of 'predictable', and over-indexed on longer term strategic planning, but I wanted to show what marketing could do when it was executing, and I wanted to prioritise the low-hanging fruit and the baseline.

This builds credibility early on. It meant that plans I produced after this were trusted.

The reality was that I spent my days executing and ticking-off the low-hanging fruit, while my evenings and weekends were dedicated to the longer term items.

Art and science

Alice De Courcy · 1st

Group Chief Marketing Officer at Cognism - Technical SaaS revenue...

2yr · 🌐

Marketers are scientists 🥼 🔬

I was speaking to James Ski and he described me as a Scientist - which is amazing, as anyone who follows Cognism or my posts will know I am all about the data.

However, it did get me thinking, marketing is also about:

✅ Being human

✅ Knowing your customer

✅ Most importantly of all - creativity

Sometimes things stop working, that's when you need to forensically analyse where the issue lies, but then, comes the creativity.

I challenged my team to get creative and throw out the playbook on how we did webinars.

The result?

See below out-take from a video they have used for our latest webinar, which, no surprise, generated 2x the number of sign ups.

Marketers need to be creative scientists! #growthmarketing

Augustinas T., Liam Bartholomew and James Sutton

😊💙👏 74   12 comments · 5 reposts

👍 Like   💬 Comment   → Share   ✈ Send

Cognism didn't run webinars before I joined the company, so I knew this was somewhere we could get ourselves a quick win.

Because we didn't have a process for webinars beforehand, we had to learn what webinars meant at Cognism.

→ What do we want them to be?

→ What was the process for running them?

→ What did we want to get out of them?

→ How did they fit into our wider marketing strategy?

In the early days, I just wanted to build muscle memory. Find our feet in terms of how we went about the process because it was foreign to the company. We didn't have the tech or the infrastructure, so that had to be our starting point.

Once we got started with a regular series, we found we could scale our content by recycling webinar content. We'd alter it for other purposes, such as in blogs or video.

This was so important for us in this early stage of our journey as a small team, and it proved to be a winning tactic.

Once we found our way through the whole webinar process, I came to the sudden realisation.

Somehow we had managed to end up running the same old playbook. We were running the webinar the way we ran everything else. Because that had been the way we had always done it.

We had a process, a cadence for webinar frequency and a clear activation checklist. All of which was being followed. But I couldn't help but think we had fallen into the trap of webinars becoming an activity we did 'just because we had always done it that way'.

Creativity and thought had gone from the process and I was left questioning the impact and role in the overall strategy.

So I wanted to change things up.

We used to care about sign-ups and attendees, that was what all the energy and effort went into.

I wanted to flip this on its head. I wanted us instead to put as much thought and concern into the quality of the content and the format of the webinars as we had been doing to driving sign-ups.
We would measure success by how many great quality snippets we could create from the webinar to use on paid and organic socials.

How many organic LinkedIn posts could be taken from the webinar.

How engaging the chat and questions were during the live event.

It's amazing how when I changed the KPIs for the team, how much better in quality the webinars became. With that, the attendees and sign-ups followed.

It was a great learning experience for me as a marketing leader to always take a step back and evaluate the 'work as normal' activities.

If you feel something can be done better then you should rethink it. Adjust your strategy in order to maximise value.

No one will prompt you to do this; it has to come from you as the marketing leader. Be honest with yourself. Continually second-guess the approaches and actions you've put in place. As well as the KPIs attached.

What is measured gets improved!

I mentioned a video in the LinkedIn post above. We created it to try to convey the value of the content that would be available in the webinar up-front.

And I feel we still have some improvements to make in this regard. Although I'm not sure any B2B organisations really do it well. But what this experiment did show us is that it can work.

The issue is it takes a lot more time and creativity.

There are still great opportunities in B2B to change the way that webinars are run. Such as:

Reward attendees

We run cold calling live sessions where we let people test out their scripts and cold calls live. And our subject matter expert coaches them on how to improve.

If they don't turn up live, they miss out on this opportunity to benefit from 1-2-1 live coaching.

Refine Labs run the following playbook. They only release the audio of their sessions. So that live attendees get to exclusively benefit from the screen-sharing content.

Showcasing value

There's still so much space to rethink how you can show people the value they can get out of attending live events.

We're collecting testimonials because we get such great dark social engagement and feedback; this is worth using for promotional purposes.

Another area of opportunity could be promotional trailers with snippets of the insights people can expect.

This is largely unexplored in the B2B world. But we all know that nowadays, video is how a lot of people consume content.

Dream team

 Alice De Courcy · 1st
Group Chief Marketing Officer at Cognism - Technical SaaS revenue...
2yr · 🌐

Scaling your marketing team - where to focus, here is my take 👇

PAID/PERFORMANCE 💸

One of my best decisions this year? Hiring an in-house dedicated performance marketer.

Someone to constantly be testing, experimenting, and building new paid campaigns to deliver SQO's.

I like to have channel experts in house, they need to be living and breathing the key metrics, only someone who has been tasting the milk daily can tell when it starts to go bad.

CONTENT 🖊

Investing early in content is always key for me. It underpins your demand gen engine, your search, and your brand.

Build a team that can form the strategy, deliver high-quality content your audience will love, all while optimising for search.

CAMPAIGNS ⛺

Our campaign execs have taken on new campaign ideation, delivering multi-channel experiments to test out new paths to SQO and beyond.

The gap I had was a need for end-to-end, multi-channel campaign delivery, and for me this role ticks that box.

PRODUCT 🎁

A vital role for me has to be your Product Marketer.

They are the voice of the customer, connecting marketing across all departments and building those all important product propositions and messages.

Who are your must-have hires? #growthmarketing

 80   10 comments

 Like   Comment   Share   Send

Paid marketing is so integral to the Cognism demand generation strategy that it's not something that we can outsource.

That being said, it can be very difficult to find the right sort of paid marketer to run this well, especially at the size of budgets and account complexity we now have at Cognism.

We split out paid into capture demand and create demand.

As part of the interview process, we soon learned that most candidates were only focused on, or only had experience in capture, not create.

To add the cherry on the cake, most of them only look at in-platform metrics as a measure of success.

Very few had experience optimising their paid activity for revenue. As well as being well versed with CRM reporting as they are at in platform reporting.

I found myself having to dig a little further into candidates' experience with:

→ Setting up accounts.
→ How they'd go about structuring data from paid platforms.
→ How they'd use UTMs for reporting within the CRM.
→ What reports and dashboards they use.

Generally, most could manage in-platform performance tracking, budget tracking and pacing through a Google sheet. They could also talk through in-platform optimisations based on MQL KPIs.

But very few were able to answer how best to track the impact of ungated content campaigns on revenue. Or how to optimise and develop a playbook for these types of 'create demand' plays on paid social.

Fewer still had the ability to give budget recommendations around the split between create and capture demand activities, or be able to provide these per platform.

These are the unicorn paid marketers, they are the ones that are worth hiring.

It has taken me two years to replace our last unicorn. During that time, we enlisted the help of the only agency I could trust with regards to running our demand playbook, Refine Labs.

Done is better than perfect

Alice De Courcy · 1st

Group Chief Marketing Officer at Cognism - Technical SaaS revenue...

2yr · 🌐

I'm a perfectionist - but in marketing, there's no time for that.

The No.1 thing I drive home the importance of with my team is that:

DONE IS BETTER THAN PERFECT

My team focuses on *tangible* results - revenue impact, generating SQOs, something visible.

We work in two-week sprints (let's leave the 'agile' discussion for another time!)

Why? 🙄

⏰ SPEED

Success in B2B SaaS is built on agility - revenue delivered, month-on-month. We only build something in the long-term if it's already proven itself in a sprint.

🗑 WASTE

Testing is part-and-parcel of revenue growth. However, the real trick is in the short-term: quick sprints to qualify whether a theory has value, and scale it from there.

🔧 PROGRESS

Over the space of two weeks, an idea turns into something concrete. It's progress. Maybe it doesn't work! Maybe you've discovered why it didn't work. Maybe you can turn it into something new? But you made progress and delivered value.

#growthmarketing

👍 55   2 reposts

👍 Like   💬 Comment   ➡ Share   ✈ Send

Ever felt decision paralysis when faced with a big question, with no immediately clear answer?

I think it's pretty common. In my experience, lots of marketers find themselves frozen by fear by the age-old question:

'How will we scale this?'

Just because there's no one single right answer.

Our competitive advantage at Cognism has been the ability to move quickly, and be one of the first in our industry to make bold moves.

I consider myself to be an action biased CMO and believe that an idea is only as good as its execution. I live and breathe this philosophy every day and it's instilled within my team.

Right now we are recreating the way B2B marketing implements demand generation. And as with anything involving stepping out into new territory, there's no instruction manual.

We don't always have all the answers. But we can't let that stop us from making progress.

We continue to test and experiment new ways of creating demand and running campaigns. Even if we don't yet have the perfect formula for measuring all of its impact.

We look for trends, we look for correlations and we collect all the data we have to make informed decisions.

It is not perfect by any means, but it's transformed our business. Moving us off the MQL hamster wheel and delivering record-breaking revenue and pipeline months.

If we were still waiting for the perfect way to measure the impact, we wouldn't be as far along as we are today.

Of course when there's so much going on, it helps to have something to manage our workflows.

We run bi-weekly sprints using Asana as our project management tool. We have boards for projects that each team is responsible for and we set milestones and KPIs against them.

By tracking projects in this way and by ensuring a regular cadence for reporting on the outcomes, it's very clear where the priorities need to be.

That's the purpose of the sprint. It's a dedicated time for us as marketing leaders to scrutinise the team's workload and focus within the context of the big picture reporting.

These insights help us to decide which activities to continue, divert or stop, depending on where our focus needs to be directed.

One of the signals we look for is increased output. It's very easy to track this if you use a project management tool like Asana and this certainly was the outcome for us when we started to work in the sprint methodology.

It's helped us to evaluate those 'because we have always done them' tasks too. This method is one of the key ways we shine a light on these types of activities and re-evaluate their utility in relation to the results.

Another benefit is the transparency into the team's workload and activities. You can clearly identify any 'busy work' from value-adding work that should be prioritised.

In the early days you don't know what is going to work. Even if you are a very experienced CMO, you don't know what will work for this unique 'coming together' of ICP, product, market fit, stage, team and more.

So you need to start to work this out fast. This is one way I've found to help me do that.

Building and getting things live quickly in the early days can be your competitive advantage. So use your experience to steer you on where to start your experimenting, and how to do it well.

Let's get it live

Alice De Courcy · 1st

Group Chief Marketing Officer at Cognism - Technical SaaS revenue...

2yr · 🌐

My favourite equation: Work in progress = no value added

How many times as a marketer have you heard:

"If we push it back a week, we could make it even better?"

That's a WHOLE WEEK of lost conversions and lost learnings.

My team is measured on things that are 'Live and adding value'. Nothing is valuable while it's a 'WIP'.

Quick experiments help you avoid wasted time. Start measuring the opportunity and time costs of delays on your work and set KPI's around this. Food for thought...

See how we track and remind ourselves of this daily 👇

#growthmarketing

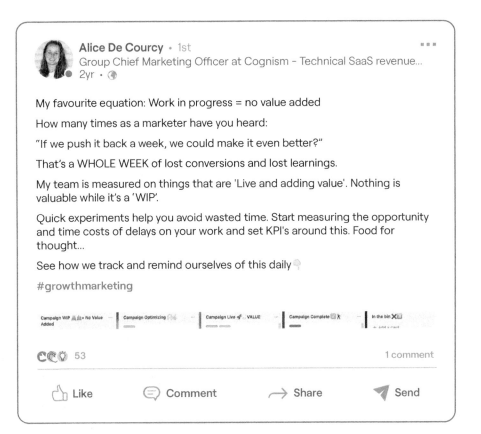

| Campaign WIP 👥👥= No Value Added | Campaign Optimizing 🔧 | Campaign Live ⚡ VALUE | Campaign Complete ❌ | In the bin ❌ |

C❤️👏 53   1 comment

👍 Like   💬 Comment   → Share   ✈ Send

WIP = no value added, ties closely to my other favourite mantra: 'done is better than perfect'.

As marketers we are notoriously good at 'busy work'. Building processes for my team which enable them to create output that always adds value has been one of my biggest challenges.

We started using Trello and weekly sprints, and now we have scaled this up to Asana and weekly sprints.

The 'how' is not the most important part of this, Google Sheets and Slack could work just as well. The main thing is creating an environment where we value output over anything else.

During our weekly sprint meetings, we'll look at our core metrics and KPIs we're driving towards. Also, looking at results from various campaigns and how our new ideas could influence or fit into the above.

Generally, it's pretty obvious to us where our next steps should be. As an example...

We recently launched what we've called 'influencer ads' on LinkedIn paid social.

Basically, we're taking screenshots of a post I might have put out on my organic LinkedIn profile, creating an ad from it - and then promoting it.

And we've seen amazing results from this in terms of CTR and number of visitors to the website. Compared to our other ads, they skyrocketed.

We decided to test out this approach because we want to engage as much as we can with people in feed. And our organic posts were performing much better than our ads. We also felt this would be a great way to get more information in front of our target audience.

From this, we decided our next best step would be to test a bespoke retargeting funnel for those people who have seen our influencer ad, in an attempt to create an aligned, personalised journey.

If we don't see an uplift in results after testing this method in a couple of weeks. Then we choose something else to test instead.

We're not going to worry about the problems around scaling it until we know it's something that works. Because getting it live and executing something is better than doing nothing.

We also have an ideas board where we add in all the things we want to test out. If we don't have an experiment on the horizon that's come out of something we're working on. Like in the example above, we'll take something out of the ideas board.

Choosing from these is a bet. You have to follow your gut and choose the one you think is going to have the biggest impact and prioritise based on that. A bit more of an art than a science.

We'd ask ourselves questions like:

→ Would it impact revenue if it worked?

→ How much effort will it involve?

→ How long would it take?

→ What possible outcome/impact could it have?

Keep in mind when you set your plan at the beginning of the quarter, you need to factor in the flexibility, time and resources to work on these experiments.

There will always be ways in which you can change, improve and expand the things you're working on.

If you stick to the plan and only the plan, you miss out on so much of the vital learning that can really drive revenue.

Some of the best stuff we've ever done has come out of experiments and remaining agile.

Tie yourself to revenue

 Alice De Courcy · 1st
Group Chief Marketing Officer at Cognism – Technical SaaS revenue...
2yr · 🌐

A new week and a new month.

It can often feel overwhelming to pick up and start all over again – a lot like looking at this blank page on my notepad over my fourth cup of tea this morning ☕.

Stay positive, look for opportunities and see it as a time for trying out new and exciting ideas.

Monday's for my team mean sprint planning and there is no better Monday than the start of a new month.

🗑 We will bin a lot today and we will learn and optimise a lot as well. 🌙

This blank page is full of opportunity!

#growthmarketing #demandgeneration #scaleups

C👏💡 53   1 comment

 Like   Comment   Share   Send

Marketers – myself included – have historically tried to avoid tying themselves to a revenue target. Or anything we can't directly influence, for that matter.

I guess because feel we don't have complete control over, why would we sign up to be responsible for it?

But, when I did take the leap and started setting goals and KPIs against revenue, everything else became a lot easier. Weirdly, the fear of missing target lessened.

I felt like I had more freedom to test out the tactics I'd been dying to try that weren't directly measurable. Because as long as they drive the end result, i.e. revenue, then that's all that matters.

I think you only get that freedom by signing up to a revenue target.

And thankfully, we've been able to hit target for the past 3+ years. Proving that all the compounding activities have made a difference. And during that time, our confidence has grown too.

But even if you did miss a month – as long as there's an upward trend across a six-month period. You can see it's having a positive effect.

So this goes out to any marketers reading who haven't committed to a revenue target. Go for it! Yes, there's pressure, but it gives you so much more flexibility in the long run. Take it as an opportunity to experiment!

Another benefit is you're taken much more seriously when speaking to the exec team. You get your seat at the table because they care about revenue. And when you're driving revenue, they're going to pay attention.

Especially if you're framing all your conversations around how your work will impact revenue. You're more likely to get the budget and resources you're asking for if you're able to tie it back to dollar amounts. Something which ultimately drives the business.

Don't dissuade yourself from setting a revenue target because of fear, or outdated beliefs about how to measure marketing success.

There are so many more doors that it can open for you as a marketing leader. And they really do outweigh the negatives.

Marrying ideas and execution

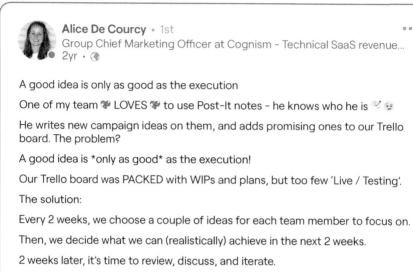

Alice De Courcy · 1st

Group Chief Marketing Officer at Cognism - Technical SaaS revenue...

2yr · 🌐

A good idea is only as good as the execution

One of my team 🐨 LOVES 🐨 to use Post-It notes – he knows who he is 😌 🙃

He writes new campaign ideas on them, and adds promising ones to our Trello board. The problem?

A good idea is *only as good* as the execution!

Our Trello board was PACKED with WIPs and plans, but too few 'Live / Testing'.

The solution:

Every 2 weeks, we choose a couple of ideas for each team member to focus on.

Then, we decide what we can (realistically) achieve in the next 2 weeks.

2 weeks later, it's time to review, discuss, and iterate.

We have become a team of MVP marketers and the output has increased hugely 💯

#growthmarketing #demandgeneration

👏💡❤️ 54   4 comments · 1 repost

👍 Like   💬 Comment   ➡️ Share   ✈️ Send

In my time as a marketer, I've noticed there tend to be three categories of person:

→ The ideas person.
→ The execution person.
→ The all-rounders.

Unfortunately, there aren't that many in the third group who combine ideas and execution. Because these people can make magic happen.

For example, when we were listening to a lot of the content from Chris Walker and Refine Labs on demand generation. We could have just shared those ideas on Slack and continued to listen and thing, 'wow, this would be great to do', but never follow through. Getting stuck in the unknown of how to execute it.

Because there wasn't a clear pathway on how to go from lead gen to demand gen - it's a daunting thing to execute. We could have just continued to do the same things.

But that would have added zero value, and we wouldn't be where we are today.

You have to take something you see, likw a good idea or a movement. And see how you can apply and implement the idea within your own business circumstances.

And what's even better is to be able to show the results at the back end too. Whether they're positive or negative, neither should block you from trying.

There tends to be a bias on people being either one way or the other, and it's less common for people to be able to marry up the two.

The way we were able to make sure we executed on our demand generation plans was to dedicate a specific workshop to it. We locked ourselves in a room for two days and worked on what we (very aptly I must say) called 'Project Find Out What Refine Labs Are Doing and Do it Better'.

I'd set everyone homework to go away and listen to all of the podcasts and read various articles and blogs. I gave everyone a week to do their demand gen research, so we could all come into the workshop with the same knowledge and understanding.

We all came together and tried to reverse-engineer what we could gather from the information we had heard.

And then we started a new project. Again, not sure how we came up with such a fabulous name... 'Project Shift How We Do Marketing'.

But we came out of the workshop with a clear set of actions, and went away and executed it. Over time our strategy has evolved as we've learned more along the way.

But I believe a lot of people would never have tried what we did because they couldn't see the exact steps to take.

Refine Labs offer the mindset and some gems of insights on how to run things. For example, setting up the conversion window on LinkedIn. So you can still report on whether people convert in a 30-day window of seeing your ungated ads. Even though you're not pushing people to a form to convert anymore. But they don't give you the play-by-play steps of what to do and how to structure it.

It does take initiative and your own creativity to come up with a model that's going to fit into your ecosystem.

We've built it in a way that makes the most sense for us and our personas. And we've continued to iterate on it as time goes on.

When there's no written playbook for how to do something, make one for yourself. Because being able to marry ideas and execution is a huge competitive advantage.

The different languages of a CMO

I certainly cannot pertain to being a linguist, or so I thought!

When it came to marketing, it became clear that each of my key stakeholders cared about very different things. So I worked hard to become fluent in CFO, CEO and VP Sales.

The things I learnt that the CFO cares about:

→ How I could help in building the bottom-up and top-down financial plans and models. This could be at the start of a new year or quarter for a new brand or a new region.

→ That I had a strong handle on my budget. So I could easily report against it and understood the importance of continued optimisations and efficiencies.

→ Understands requirements for sustainable growth and someone who will question all spend against the projected ROI and opportunity cost. You need to be able to show your ability to scrutinise costs and bring proposals for cost savings to the table.

Things I learnt that the CEO cares about:

→ In every 1-2-1 with my CEO I start with an update on where we are against my plan. I highlight any risk areas, for which I will have a plan of attack ready and prepared.

→ My CEO is also passionate about our people and that is a critical element for how he measures my success. Have I been building a happy team of high-performing marketers that are scaling with the company?

→ CEO's are entrepreneurs and they always want to be innovating. Especially in marketing. Marketing changes more than any other discipline and with this it is vital that you can show a pattern of consistent innovation and commitment to excellence.

→ Finally, scaling the brand really matters. There is no one in the company that the brand matters to more than the CEO. They will have a clear feeling for how this is evolving under your leadership and you should be prepared to show the impact of this as well.

And don't forget your revenue counterpart, your work-wife or husband, the VP Sales.

Now I could write a whole book on this topic alone, but will keep this short!

Your VP Sales cares about:

→ How you are enabling their reps and them to hit the revenue plan? How much are you contributing in revenue and pipeline? And how much effort is it taking their reps to convert this?

→ They are laser focused on their reps ability to hit quota. Anything marketing can do to help with this will be well received. That could be improving conversion rates at various stages throughout the funnel, or even writing the contents of their cadences for them.

→ The types of projects that you should work on with your VP Sales are things which have a clear path to more revenue or efficiency. Examples of this could be direct to AE routing, or inbound grading and routing.

Once you get fluent in all these languages, your role as CMO becomes a little bit easier.

You can start to tailor your approach in meetings based on this knowledge, presenting data and reporting in the corresponding ways.

This was a big unlock for me, and while the people in the seats may change, the expectations and motivations tend to remain very stable.

CFO language	CEO language	VP Sales language
Financial planning and modeling	Revenue plan	Revenue plan
Budgeting	Happy and scaling team	Sales capacity / quota achievement
Efficiency	Innovation	Revenue focused experiments / levers
Controlled growth	Scaling brand	

Give yourself problems

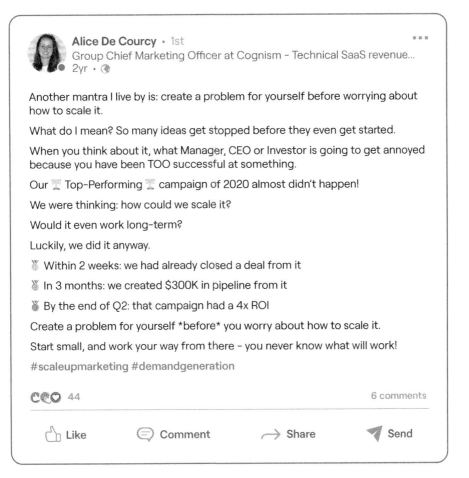

Alice De Courcy · 1st · · ·
Group Chief Marketing Officer at Cognism - Technical SaaS revenue...
2yr · 🌐

Another mantra I live by is: create a problem for yourself before worrying about how to scale it.

What do I mean? So many ideas get stopped before they even get started.

When you think about it, what Manager, CEO or Investor is going to get annoyed because you have been TOO successful at something.

Our 🏆 Top-Performing 🏆 campaign of 2020 almost didn't happen!

We were thinking: how could we scale it?

Would it even work long-term?

Luckily, we did it anyway.

🥇 Within 2 weeks: we had already closed a deal from it

🥈 In 3 months: we created $300K in pipeline from it

🥉 By the end of Q2: that campaign had a 4x ROI

Create a problem for yourself *before* you worry about how to scale it.

Start small, and work your way from there - you never know what will work!

#scaleupmarketing #demandgeneration

🅒🅒💚 44   6 comments

👍 Like   💬 Comment   → Share   ✈ Send

We didn't offer a free trial at Cognism, we only offered demo requests.

But we wanted to diversify our offers and let people experience our product hands-on so they could see the value up front.

So we came up with this idea of '25 free leads', where we could offer people 25 leads in their ICP for free.

They would get a sample of the types of contacts we had to offer in their ICP and be able to understand the quality of our data without having to commit yet.

I got this idea approved by our CRO with the only stipulation being we couldn't run this as a mass offer to everyone. It had to be a super-tight audience at first.

I just wanted to validate that this idea would even work and was an offer our audience cared about.

So we kept the audience size really small at first. It was only retargeting people who had already engaged with us and knew a bit about Cognism.

We put it live and saw amazing results. Not only were people converting on the offer but they were converting into revenue further down the funnel.

It became our top-performing campaign by a mile.

At that stage, we knew it worked. So we had an argument for scaling it. We then just had to figure out how.

I believe it's a much better position to be in, instead of worrying about how to scale it later on. And then giving up before even trying it out.

All too often we block ourselves from trying ideas because we can't imagine how we would scale them. For example, we could have said:

'There's no way we can deal with 200 requests for 25 free leads a month, how would we resource it.'

And not go ahead with it. But that would have been the wrong decision.

I think it was great that we tested it before we knew how we could scale it. Because we proved that it worked.

Then it was easy to get buy-in to build more robust processes around it, because it was driving revenue. You could see it in the numbers.

This can be a mindset shift for some people, because what happens if we can't fulfil what we set out to? Of course, people want to do things to a high standard, and that's a good thing most of the time.

But to make the right decisions fast, you need to be creating minimal viable tests and minimal viable products. To find out if it's the right direction to push in.

It's just a new way of thinking about things. Don't worry about a problem that doesn't yet exist.

Align your destinies

 Alice De Courcy · 1st   • • •
Group Chief Marketing Officer at Cognism - Technical SaaS revenue...
2yr · 🌐

When sales and marketing are aligned and you get feedback like this from your MDR team lead on a Wednesday AM 🤝

The secret sauce to repeatable marketing success...MDR's and a content engine that works.

We have an amazing team of MDR experts in Callum McManus, Sam Gibbons, Derek Howard Leckner, and our awesome leader Evangeline Crossland.

#demandgeneration #growthmarketing

> **Evangeline Crossland** 11:47
> Hey both, just some feedback, some unreal leads this morning. Like super relevant job titles, industries, geographies! First cold call I made today I booked in!

👍❤️👏 67   4 comments

👍 Like   💬 Comment   → Share   ✈ Send

Alright – I know I've said this a couple times already... but obviously we moved away from a lead gen approach towards demand gen.

But when we were using lead gen, we had the best possible playbook.

So if you are in a smaller company or startup, and want to run the lead gen playbook then here are some tips.

100% have dedicated sales reps who know and understand:

→ The content you're producing.
→ The different types of calls you need to make on the back of that content.
→ Focused only on dealing with these types of leads.

I wrote this post originally because, at the time, our focus was on getting quality content leads into the funnel for our MDRs to work.

And the main reason that we were so successful with our MDRs was because our destinies were so aligned.

For both sales and marketing to succeed, we had to be driving towards the same outcomes.

One of our KPIs was around the conversion rate between the content lead to sales qualified opportunity, and we were working to increase that.

It had been hanging around the 5% mark and we wanted to push it up to 10%.

By having MDRs in place who specialised in content and by having really close feedback loops. For example, listening to the types of conversations our MDRs were having off the back of various pieces of content. We were able to push that information back into the content engine.

Using this process, we pushed our conversion rate up to between 11% and 15%. I believe we made it as efficient as you can for what I'll call 'cold lead gen'. I feel that we nailed that process.

Key things for us to find scalable and repeatable success were:

→ Having a dedicated MDR role.
→ Having them work closely with the marketing function (especially with feedback on content).
→ Having aligned KPIs and working towards the same goals.
→ Feeling as though you're responsible for each other's success. For example, the marketing team had a responsibility to the MDRs and vice versa.

Because we found feedback to be crucial in this process, we had weekly calls with the MDRs and the MDR manager.

We'd run through all of the key stats like:

→ Conversion rates.

→ The length of time between lead download and follow up (we found a strong correlation between a shorter gap between downloads and contacting prospects and higher quality conversations!) Within 48 hours was the sweet spot.

→ Qualitative feedback based on what's learned during calls (for example, we learned our MDRs found pitching off the back of a cold calling handbook download was easier versus our content marketing playbook.)

→ Number of actionable leads per MDR. We signed up to 400 per MDR per month, as this gave them the capacity they needed to hit their MB targets based on current conversions rates.

These meetings were also a great opportunity to flag when MDRs felt low on leads. Or another part of the process wasn't working. That often meant we never went a month without realising that one of our processes wasn't working well. Causing a chaotic run around to fix or catch up!

Providing value

 Alice De Courcy · 1st
Group Chief Marketing Officer at Cognism - Technical SaaS revenue...
2yr · 🌐

•••

Following Dave Gerhardt and sharing who my first three marketing hires for a new team would be 🪴

The main thing for me when starting a new team is that you work with, and hire, people you trust. These team members are so crucial, you can't afford to make a mistake.

Make sure that rolodex is kept up-to-date!

#growthmarketing #demandgeneration

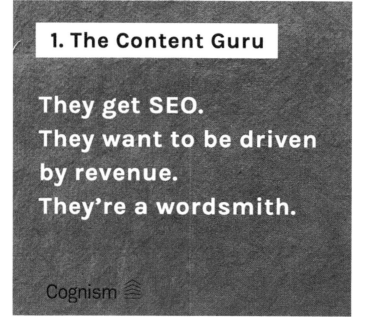

🖐💗❤ 51   5 comments

👍 Like   💬 Comment   ➡ Share   ✈ Send

You hopefully (!!!) have noticed throughout this diary so far that I've always been quite keen to provide value in my LinkedIn posts.

And this wasn't necessarily a strict strategy at first, in fact it wasn't a strategy at all. I just wanted to share my experiences with people on LinkedIn in case it helped them.

I did make the decision to create more of a content strategy around my posts. But only after learning more about how we could leverage subject matter experts and I saw the value in using LinkedIn as an organic channel for distribution. I realised I was becoming a channel that I could use to Cognism's benefit.

I started off by emulating some of the content formats I enjoyed from other LinkedIn creators. Then I kept an eye on what seemed to go down well with my audience.

Over the past year or so, I've over doubled my follower count and boosted the engagement on my posts, which is great!

One thing I'd urge people to do if you want to build your own personal brand to help boost your company's reach, is to not worry too much about it being perfect.

Some of my old posts have typos (that my husband would take great satisfaction in pointing out to me!) But honestly, I don't care about that.

I wanted my posts to be authentic. And I don't want to hold back for fear of mis-typing or having perfect graphics.

If I have a thought about something I want to share, I just share it. That might mean I'm typing it out while on a train, during my lunchtime dog walk, or in a five-minute gap between meetings.

As long as the content you're posting is valuable, no one cares about the typos. You might get the odd snide comment about spelling - although I never have - but who cares? You can go back and edit your post if you want to.

So don't overthink it.

The other big piece of advice I give to my team is that everyone has something to share that is valuable to an audience out there. It doesn't matter how senior you are or how long you have been in a role. You will be learning every day, and this learning can be a cheat code for others, so share it.

Cognism DNA

 Alice De Courcy · 1st
Group Chief Marketing Officer at Cognism – Technical SaaS revenue...
2yr · 🌐

Marketing kick off 2021 🏉

🎯 How are we going to achieve our targets?

Here are the principles that will guide us through 2021:

1️⃣ Efficiency – waving a happy farewell to lengthy campaign plans that take months to execute only to flop. We have fully embraced a campaign sprint methodology.

2️⃣ Transparency – we are still working from home, & everyone is getting lots done, but it's difficult to see sometimes. So in 2021 we are going to share everything, this will inevitably lead to better idea flow.

3️⃣ Innovation + ownership + execution: queue mantra: 'a good idea is only as good as its execution'.

4️⃣ Revenue marketing: own, know, love the numbers. We are building a team of revenue focused marketers, 'scientists' .

And our purpose for being:

'Make sales easier' Jonathon Ilett, Kristapor Giragosian – you will like that one!

#growthmarketing #demandgeneration

👍❤️👏 66   8 comments

👍 Like   💬 Comment   ➡️ Share   ✈️ Send

In marketing kick-offs, I like to highlight certain characteristics that have helped us to be successful so far. These are things I'd like new members of the team to inherit as we scale, and older members of the team to remember.

I want these to be a part of our DNA and philosophy as a marketing department as we move forward and scale.

At this point, we had just added new members to the team. And I realised I needed to invest more of my time to defining processes that would drive these critical principles within the team.

We had to get out of the startup mentality. We had to stop getting stuff done by hacking things together using a small number of very hands-on people, who're laser focused on shipping value. Instead, we had to move towards a more process-driven approach so we could continue to scale.

1. Efficiency

We had reached a point where we had more people in the team, but we were less efficient with those people. So it came down to myself and the other managers to take responsibility and make this a key focus. It wasn't the responsibility of the new starters..

More than anything it a reflection of the stage of growth we were at. But it was also something I felt was important to pay attention to throughout the year.

There will be a point of scale where you have to set time aside to build out processes and infrastructure that will enable the team to be more effective and efficient with scale. The short term hit on output while you build these out can be painful, but this is the only way to build for sustainable growth.

2. Transparency

During this time, we had been working from home for a while because of the pandemic. And even now, a lot of our marketing team is remote.

While I have my direct reports keeping me updated with progress, these people also have their own teams. So I can end up being quite far removed from a lot of the day-to-day work that gets done.

I'm sure it feels a bit arduous for those who are in the details, working hard to then have to add an update to their to-do list. But it's important, not only for me, but the whole team to keep up to date with projects. I believe that's where creative ideas are born.

We have so many smart people - you never know what creative ideas could come out of sharing what the team is up to.

We had become a little siloed and a bit too focused on our own work.

This was my push to try to bring back a level of transparency within the team.

I ran incentives about sharing and I told my team, 'this is the easiest money you will ever win because all you have to do is share your work'. Sometimes you just have to incentivise the behaviour you want until it becomes a part of the way you operate.

3. Innovation, ownership and execution

This comes back to one of my favourite phrases:

'Ideas are only as good as their execution.'

What I was trying to get at is that I want people to come up with solutions to problems, not just problems that need solutions. And I want us to be able to execute that.

It comes down to empowering the team to take ownership of certain projects, and say to them. 'Please come to me with a fully-formed plan of action around how you think we could do something better'.

Because I would love to help my team get an action live, whatever that test looks like.

Ideally I want those ideas and plans to come from everyone in my team, not just managers.

That was the secret sauce for our success in the early days. We came up with some great ideas and I didn't want that to get lost as we grew the team.

It is easy to fall into the trap of team members looking to their managers for direction and ideation and that is the death of innovation.

4. Revenue marketing

I feel it's super important for everyone in my team to know what the key metrics are.

Whether they're in SEO, whether they're in content, whether they're in demand gen. We all drive towards revenue.

That's the number one goal of our marketing team.
It's important for everyone to be working on something that can positively influence the growth of the company and ultimately results in increasing revenue.

That means we all have to be very involved in the data and this is an area where I want the team to maintain focus.

These principles came from me observing the team, looking ahead at our growth plans and prioritising past competitive advantages that led us to success so far. They were the key elements of our team's DNA that I wanted to solidify.

Another thing I just want to touch on here before I move on - as I mention it in this post, but haven't really spoken about it in this diary so far - working from home.

Marketing is lucky as a discipline in the sense that it can be done from anywhere, and a lot of our team continues to work remotely or on a flexible basis.

I do feel that the team can benefit from being in the same room, even just to discuss options for the subject line of an email easily and quickly. So we do get together when we can.

We also did suffer initially from issues discussed in my previous points (efficiency and transparency) which is why I made those two areas a focus.

But I feel it's the role of a leader to do all they can to remove silos and create processes that make it possible to be productive in whatever environment is required.

We've now found our flow with processes and developed our mindset and philosophy around working from home which offers the team a lot more flexibility and work-life balance, without any negative cost to productivity.

We've also experienced massive benefits from being able to hire talent from further afield which I feel has outweighed the negatives we experienced in the beginning.

LinkedIn wins

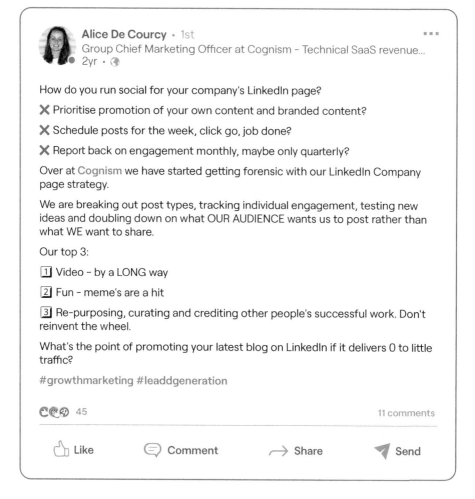

We've always had our LinkedIn page sit with the content team. After all, if we want to provide our audience with quality content, then who better to provide them with that?

What's been key for us has been to have a dedicated team member focused on the details of what's working, and what's not. Having a very data-driven mentality.

While I think we've found our groove with our LinkedIn page now, we did find it difficult to transition towards a value-led approach initially because we were still taking requests from other areas of the business.

For example, sharing promos on an upcoming partnership webinar.

But once we had drawn up a clear strategy document for our company's LinkedIn page and firmly established road rules around what could be posted, and what couldn't – it was much easier.

Our rule of thumb on our LinkedIn page is:

Anything that doesn't provide direct value in the post doesn't get on the page.

Because before, when someone would ask if we could just pop this on LinkedIn, we'd just do it. We didn't have a reason to say no.

But now, we have clear guidelines. We can say 'this wouldn't benefit the overall strategy of our company page, nor would it impact any of the KPIs set, so no, we won't post this'.

Or we can suggest an alternative, for example maybe it's something better suited to be targeted towards a specific audience on paid social.

One thing to add here is that I've mentioned we use memes in this post. But we don't anymore. We found that memes left too much to the imagination. Memes that we felt were funny and innocent were interpreted differently by other people so we decided it was best to avoid them in most cases so we didn't inadvertently negatively impact our brand.

We could maintain our growth trajectory without them. The main thing is to focus on value each and every time.

Another helpful thing I can't recommend enough is repurposing content. But not just any content. Use the data you have access to.

Look at your top-performing blogs and repurpose those into a relevant content format, such as a carousel.

Look at your comments – what are the most common things people ask questions about? Use that to build your posts around.

And don't forget once your posts are live, use the data at your fingertips to learn more about what people respond to.
While we were still in our lead gen phase when I wrote this post. You can see this was the beginning of our demand gen thinking.

We wanted to create an audience of our own so we didn't have to be so reliant on other people. We'd seen Gong create this strong channel for themselves and we knew we wanted the same.

We wanted to get into the media machine mindframe. Which we've only continued to build out since.

Minimal viable product

 Alice De Courcy · 1st
Group Chief Marketing Officer at Cognism – Technical SaaS revenue...
2yr · 🌐

Build the demand and AFTER build to scale it.

This is by far my best tip for all marketers looking to test new ways to grow.

Some examples of how you can do this:

Create a landing page, and offer, test it through paid for traction.

Restrict the audience to re-targeting if you need to control for volume, or market an 'early bird' incentive if it's something you haven't built/created yet and you want to check for demand before you do.

Your boss/CEO isn't going to get annoyed because you have generated TOO much demand for an offer/tool/incentive.

SO don't get stuck on an idea because you don't know how to scale it right now.

#demandgeneration #growthmarketing

 49   5 comments

👍 Like   💬 Comment   ➦ Share   ✈ Send

I wish I could say I'd come up with this philosophy myself, but this was one I'd learned in a previous role working in an early-stage startup.

The product team operated a very lean, MVP first approach and I had very minimal resources to work with. So I'd adopted this way of thinking and found it to be a useful approach to get things done and start learning quickly.

So when it came to experimenting at Cognism, I followed this same philosophy.

For example, in the old lead gen days, before creating a long-form content asset I would often launch an early-bird sign up landing page to see how much traction and demand there was for the asset.

It was a great way to validate the topic and idea before investing weeks writing and creating it.

Otherwise you could end up wasting a whole lot of time and effort working on something that no one was interested in to start with.

Another example that springs to mind was when we were creating a tool for our 'ROI' calculator.

We started with a simple Excel doc.

Once we knew people were using it, we could validate the use case. Plus, we then had some UX feedback we could work with to make it a tool people would find valuable.

That was our signal to invest in building a more robust tool to serve the need.

As I've said before in this diary, it's better to create problems for yourself than to never try.

So just think about what your MVP could look like. What's the minimal test you can run to prove your theory? Then worry about scaling that later.

I used this same logic when producing this diary. As you can see in the LinkedIn post below, I asked how people would most enjoy consuming a piece of content like this - as you can see, it's pretty long!

The reception was really encouraging and served as validation for our ideas on how we would activate the asset when we launched it.

It gave us a lot of confidence to continue to invest time and resources in creating a robust plan for the diary's distribution.

Alice De Courcy · 1st

Group Chief Marketing Officer at Cognism – Technical SaaS revenue...

2 mo · 🌐

Diary of a first time CMO.

We are working on something...

It's going to be an open and honest account of my time as a first time CMO.

Over indexing on actionable and tactical insights that we hope will be helpful.

My aim: help others through giving away what's worked and being honest about what hasn't.

BUT...it's getting long!

So I'd love to hear from you how you would like to consume this, and even if you would consume it?

Audio? Video? Long form text post? PDF (joking – unless you want that!)?

Please comment and let me know if

1. You would even want a resource like this?

2. How you would want to consume it?

#b2bmarketing #demandgeneration

Diary of a first time CMO

Introduction

Entry 1: Put yourself in their shoes

Entry 2: Test your boundaries

Entry 3: Lessons I've learned about marketing and sales alignment

Lesson 1: Growing a team

Entry 4: Data is everything

Entry 5: Lessons from E-books

Entry 6: Quality over quantity

Entry 7: Value customer loyalty

Entry 8: CMO of a startup

Entry 9: Day 1 and a marketing leader

Entry 10: Cut the BS

492   97 comments · 1 repost

 Like   Comment   Share   Send

B2B marketing doesn't have to be boring

Alice De Courcy · 1st

Group Chief Marketing Officer at Cognism - Technical SaaS revenue...

2yr · 🌐

Do you give your team enough room to get creative?

I was reminded yesterday why at Cognism we aim to avoid 'copy and paste' marketing.

Below email credit to Liam Bartholomew - this is a snippet from one of his 'closed lost' email nurture programmes.

And this is only 1 of the amazing responses we have had from it, not to mention rejuvenated opps and deals.

If we limit ourselves and our teams to 'best practices', or 'go and see what our competition or other SaaS marketers are doing' narratives, we reduce our chances of success and finding and building a truly unfair competitive advantage.

How much room do you give your team to try and test new things?

How much time do you dedicate to coming up with innovative ideas?

#b2bmarketing #leadgeneration #saasmarketing

Sure, we can be friends... 😊

Just FYI - I shared this with our marketing department because it made me laugh. Usually I roll my eyes at emails like this but this one was perfect.

Loved your platform, your sales reps, everything. It was just too expensive for our little company.

From: Cognism <marketing@cognism.com>
Sent: Monday, March 1, 2021 4:03 AM
To:
Subject: Sure, we can be friends... 😊

When they say "We're just friends" but you already planned out your life with them

🧡💬❤ 54   3 comments · 2 reposts

👍 Like   💬 Comment   ↱ Share   ✈ Send

If you want to stand out in the marketing game, you need to be doing things differently. Giving your team the space and freedom to be creative is so important for this reason. It could be the difference between a new best performing campaign and, well... the same old humdrum.

But at the same time, you need to have guardrails in place that ensure people know where the boundaries are. This might sound like the opposite of creative freedom, but it's more about maintaining your brand and output. This isn't marketers gone wild after all!

So I like to think of my guidelines as a bit of a brand book, filled with examples to spark ideas and provide more understanding.

As a marketing organisation we are trying to change the way B2B marketers do marketing. We live and breathe the motto that B2B marketing doesn't have to be boring! This means it has to become a part of the team's DNA and is ingrained in everything we do.

We challenge ourselves by asking, 'is there a better way to do this?'

Or are we just doing it because 'it has always been done that way'?

We reward creative ideas. We reward those who can execute those creative ideas. We showcase the amazing work that is produced. And we operate with a very flat hierarchy.

I feel it's been our competitive advantage. We've been able to stand out from the crowd of B2B companies because we don't do the, 'same old same old'. We want to be the opposite of a boring B2B business.

One of the signs I've noticed that tells me it's working is we're always being tagged in posts, almost daily now, that call us a B2B brand doing things differently.

You certainly get the first-mover advantage if you are brave and bold, trying to do things differently.

Whether that be making the jump from an MQL model, running e-books and content downloads, to rethinking the way traditional email nurtures function (think Netflix but for email nurture!)

Or taking a leaf out of Bumble's advertising playbook and leaning into positively advertising your competition.

The amazing thing about marketing is that your work is never done. There's always a new idea out there that you can test, you just need to be able to deliver it.

View from a distance

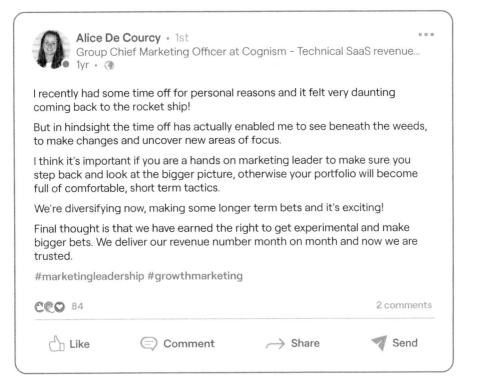

Alice De Courcy · 1st

Group Chief Marketing Officer at Cognism - Technical SaaS revenue...

1yr · 🌐

I recently had some time off for personal reasons and it felt very daunting coming back to the rocket ship!

But in hindsight the time off has actually enabled me to see beneath the weeds, to make changes and uncover new areas of focus.

I think it's important if you are a hands on marketing leader to make sure you step back and look at the bigger picture, otherwise your portfolio will become full of comfortable, short term tactics.

We're diversifying now, making some longer term bets and it's exciting!

Final thought is that we have earned the right to get experimental and make bigger bets. We deliver our revenue number month on month and now we are trusted.

#marketingleadership #growthmarketing

🤟❤️ 84   2 comments

👍 Like   💬 Comment   ➡️ Share   ✈️ Send

You might be wondering why it felt so daunting for me to come back after a short break away from work. Afterall, I'm the CMO. A leader... I should be confident and unwavering, right?

Truth is because Cognism is at such a high-growth stage, everything changes at a rapid rate. Re-entering after a period of time off can feel like you don't know where to start.

You need to throw yourself back in and get up to speed, especially as a hands-on leader who is used to being very operational.

BUT this was actually just what I needed.

Sometimes you can't see the wood for the trees, and it is only by taking a step back and looking at your organisation as a whole that you can identify opportunity areas and also have space to be creative and form new ideas.

Ultimately you will have got to this role because you are very good at marketing. Not because of your people or org management ability. You need the space to think proactively about this from time to time to ensure you are still having the required impact.

I'm not saying it's easy either, I find it really hard to take breaks. Even on my honeymoon, much to my husband's dismay!

I feel incredibly invested in everything that I've built during my nearly four years here. From my team of 3, now approaching 40. Delivering consistent month-on-month, quarter-on-quarter marketing revenue growth. And Cognism expansion, now being three brands.

But it's really important to give others the chance to step-up and lead.

One of the main things I had time to mull over during my time off was the growing pains we'd started to experience due to our quick growth.

I had the space to look at how I could operationalise our processes and find ways of working to enable us to move faster and build and scale for the future.

This can get lost when you move fast and grow quickly, but if you are going to hit the next level of growth, they become vitally important.

It also gave me a chance to think about the bigger picture of how we foundationally operated.

To start to look and ideate on how I could potentially switch Cognism from a lead generation model into a demand generation one.

I started to map out what I would need to begin this process, for example:

→ An experimentation budget.
→ Buy-in internally.

And I did a huge amount of listening and learning, something I don't usually get the time for. I was beginning to work out how this could play out in real life.

I often wonder if I had not had this head space and time, if I would have been able to make the switch when we did and as successfully as we did. I guess we'll never know.

Switching gears

 Alice De Courcy · 1st
Group Chief Marketing Officer at Cognism - Technical SaaS revenue...
1yr · 🌐

In my marketing team I hired an SDR, a CSM & a Client Sequence Writer...

These were all internal hires and they all now work in very different, but very core roles within the marketing team.

SDR 🔄 Performance Marketing Manager

CSM 🔄. Content and SEO Exec

Client Sequence Writer 🔄. First and currently sole Product Marketer

They are all phenomenal at their roles, but none of them had 'direct marketing role experience' before.

What they had was more important, and it enabled them to outshine external candidates in the interview stages...

They knew our customers and prospects inside out, working with them daily.

Do we overestimate the experience required for a marketing role and therefore are we overlooking the value that other internal customer facing roles could bring to marketing?

How many 'non marketers' have you hired?

In what roles?

#leadgeneration #b2bmarketingstrategy

👍❤️😊 76   7 comments

👍 Like   💬 Comment   ➡ Share   ✈ Send

If you're hiring someone externally, you have to be aware that you're bringing someone on board who has all the skills to execute the role - but almost zero understanding of your customer or business.

And unfortunately, what they're lacking is what can make them hugely valuable to your organisation, and it can take them a considerable amount of time to get up to speed.

For certain roles, for example a website manager, that's fine - they don't need to know much about the ins and outs of who your ICP is.

But for other roles, that's crucial information.

At the time when we made these hires, we simply didn't have time at our disposal. We needed to do things quickly. I felt I could teach our internal hires the marketing piece much faster than I could teach all the nuances of our customer and product.

And it presented a great opportunity for us to live and breathe one of our core values which is to promote internally wherever possible.

And I'd 100% make this decision again.

Our client sequence writer who we promoted to Product Marketer, went on to become our Head of Product Marketing.

She's become invaluable, her deep understanding of the product and our customers would make her a very difficult person to replace. Should she ever choose to move on from Cognism.

The SDR who stepped into Performance Marketing stayed with us for the next two years, before then leaving to start his own business utilising the performance marketing skills he had learned, which is amazing.

And our CSM, who became an SEO and Content Exec, became one of the strongest SEO Execs we've ever had.

All three of these hires were hugely successful and each of them have gone on to further develop skills in the areas they were hired into.

CMO stands for 'Change Means Opportunities'

Alice De Courcy · 1st
Group Chief Marketing Officer at Cognism – Technical SaaS revenue...
1yr · 🌐

Don't measure an eBook's success by the number of MQL's it generates...

Success of an eBook should be measured by how many people speak to your sales reps about the quality of the content.

Wise words from Chris Walker when I chatted to him last year about everything eBook's.

How do you measure the success of your long form content right now?

A firm lover of eBooks and gated content (done well), I have slowly been moving some of my chips into brand and the early signs are positive.

Are you open to change as a marketer? How brave are you willing to be?

#leadgeneration #demandgeneration

MEASURING CONTENT SUCCESS WITH CHRIS WALKER

🤚👍 28   5 comments

👍 Like   💬 Comment   ➡ Share   ✈ Send

We never really measured the success of any long-form content based on the number of MQLs it generated. Even before we had this conversation with Chris Walker.

Instead, we'd focus on the number of MQLs that converted into SQOs.

We found that measuring this helped us to understand how easy it was for our reps to have conversations with people who had downloaded content.

We always wanted to focus on the quality of the content.. I guess that's why it wasn't that big of a jump in mindset to consider demand generation.

But at this stage, while I was definitely thinking about it, we hadn't made the switch over to a demand generation model yet.

That's what I'm referring to when I mention 'moving chips towards brand', as it was us really starting to look at how we could experiment with how demand generation could work for us.

One of the first things I did in this process was to ask our CEO for a 5k budget that I could use to experiment activating a DG playbook with.

For example, we ungated some of our best-performing content and ran it in an ungated way on paid social. And at the same time, I was looking to see if I could find a correlation between the spend on ungated content ads and direct in-bounds increasing month over month.

We ran this experiment for about four months, and every month, the number of inbounds we had were increasing in-line with our DG activity. I knew there was something in this.

One important thing to remember when you're a CMO is you have to be open to change. I would never have made the move to this successful mindset shift if I weren't open to the idea of change.

In all honesty, I don't think anyone could work at Cognism unless you were open to the idea of change because things move so quickly around here.

And to go wider still, if you're going to be good at marketing – then you need to accept that the world of marketing is ever evolving.

To be successful, you have to be willing to experiment and consider making changes. Quickly too – if you want to have a first-mover advantage rather than copying what everyone else is doing.

I love ideas. I love experiments. I embrace change. And I really hope that's something I've built into the DNA of my team.

Recognition and rewards

Alice De Courcy · 1st　　　　　　　　　　　　· · ·
Group Chief Marketing Officer at Cognism - Technical SaaS revenue...
2yr · 🌐

Looking back on what is approaching a 2 year journey at Cognism so far, tasked with taking marketing from scattergun, in-person event heavy, to a predictable engine that can be dialled up and down.

Last night I watched our marketing dashboard break all records to end Q1.

We ended 190% of our marketing revenue target in the UK and 169% globally!

Better than this, we now see consistent predictability in our channels.

Lots more work still to be done, we start today back on 0 and go again!

But sometimes its good to look back, reflect and celebrate!

Only possible with a superstar team: Liam Bartholomew, Augustinas T., Joe Barron, Fran Langham, Vera Kalinn (Verche Karafıloska), Di Frost, Ilse V Rensburg, Oscar Frost, Ashleigh Frank, Nicole Peters, Emma Sexton, James Sutton, Emily Liu, Ognen Bojkovski, Greig Kaj Robertson

#leadgeneration #demandgeneration

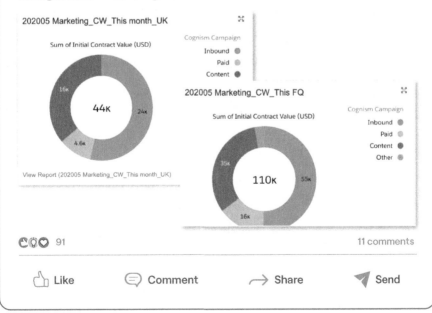

❤️👏😮 91　　　　　　　　　　　　　　　　　　　11 comments

👍 Like　　　　💬 Comment　　　　➡️ Share　　　　✈️ Send

It's important to take a moment, once in a while, to reflect on all your hard work as a team.

We can sometimes get caught up in the day-to-day, and forget that we've made such huge progress. We've actually just had another record breaking Q3, but even still, we have to be planning ahead for Q4.

So it's hard to just stop and take stock, but this was a big moment. Another reminder that we were achieving the main goal we had been set. Which was building a predictable revenue model through marketing.

And we couldn't have done it without each and every one of our team members.

At the end of the day, what makes your company or marketing org successful is the people. And I always want to recognise hard work, dedication and achievements.

Us having a record-breaking quarter at this stage of growth was massive, and I wanted to recognise everyone in the team for their contribution.

Shoutouts in general have been built into the way we work. We have a Slack channel dedicated to doing just that, and we post in it daily.

We also nominate someone from the team to be 'marketer of the week' based on nominations from across the team.

Basically, any opportunity we get to celebrate the good work everyone's doing, we try to do it. Especially now that we have a much larger team and we are remote.

I wouldn't want anyone to feel as though their work is going unnoticed or they don't know how they're contributing to our wider company goals.

I think that helps to make Cognism a nice place to be, where people feel valued. I think this is key to having a team who are motivated to perform at their best every day.

And their best helped us to achieve what you can see in the screenshot above.

Our sources of revenue were inbound, paid and content. At this time we were still running the lead gen play - and content (by this we mean the gated e-book downloads) was making up a significant section of the pie.

This was a huge success, we had created three predictable channels where we could scale and hit revenue targets. The CFO, CRO and CEO loved it.

I've talked a fair bit about our old lead gen process so far in this diary, so I won't go too into detail again. But here's a few things I think were the keys to our success:

- → Our dedicated MDRs.
- → Focusing on quality content.
- → Being revenue focused.
- → We were scientific and mathematical.
- → We tied our destinies closely together with our MDRs.

All of these things helped this to become a very successful motion for us at this scale and stage of growth.

Another thing worth mentioning here is that you can see our inbounds make up for a large proportion of the graph, and I think the reason for this is because we invested really early on in SEO and content in general, outside of just gated e-books.

The compounding effect of these content investments has been huge. It was one of the best bets we could have made early doors.

It might feel like a hard choice to make when you're first starting out because you won't see the full outcome until much further on down the line - but it's so worth it. Invest in content.

Experimental budget

 Alice De Courcy · 1st
Group Chief Marketing Officer at Cognism – Technical SaaS revenue...
1yr · 🌐

Demand Generation Marketing is a game of poker.

You need to place your bets. The key is being able to balance short term with long term plays.

And learning to live with imperfection is key.

At any one time there will be 100s of things that could be improved:

- that copy on a webpage that gets less than 50 views a month
- an email nurture flow that hasn't been touched in 2 months
- a new speaker for your podcast to source, meet and record

Your success will be directly tied to how you priorities these tasks and how you push back and pause those things that can remain imperfect while you focus on moving the needle with other 'key moves'.

Real example: A month or so ago we paused our 'to do list'.

We decided to take a bet on brand and get live a whole range of our best performing content, promoted free to access on paid social to our core personas.

The results: 30% uplift in direct inbounds.

But that webpage still gives me shivers and that nurture 'could be better'.

#growthmarketing #demandgeneration

👏👍❤️ 106   17 comments · 2 reposts

👍 Like   💬 Comment   → Share   ✈️ Send

This is where things get juicy.

After 33 entries in the diary, we are finally making the move towards demand generation.

I remember a while ago, I was doing a podcast and my guest was talking about how they had an experimental budget that didn't need to be tied back to revenue. It was simply a budget to test ideas with.

And I thought that was a brilliant idea. I had so many ideas for how I wanted to experiment with demand generation to get the ball rolling, so why not ask for an experimental line?

Turns out it wasn't much of a fight to get it either.

Because we had just proven our predictable marketing engine, hitting all of our revenue targets. The CFO and CEO had no problems giving me a budget of 5k to play with.

I'd recommend any CMO ask for the same. As it was this budget that gave me the freedom to explore ideas, find what DG tactics worked for us, and meant I had data to back-up my decisions.

I was pretty bought into the whole demand generation idea by now. I just needed the time and budget to scale out how it would look at Cognism.

How could we create and deliver valuable, ungated, 'always on' content to our ideal customer persona? And would I continue to see an uplift in inbounds as a result? Would this increase bridge the gap that would be left by no longer running the content playbook?

I think the reason I found this budget so revolutionary because I felt we had so many options. So many ideas. So many opportunities. How did we narrow down what we did next?

Well, this offered us a way to prioritise.

Humans marketing to humans

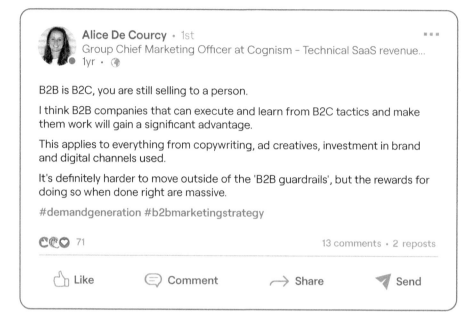

Alice De Courcy · 1st
Group Chief Marketing Officer at Cognism – Technical SaaS revenue...
1yr · 🌐

B2B is B2C, you are still selling to a person.

I think B2B companies that can execute and learn from B2C tactics and make them work will gain a significant advantage.

This applies to everything from copywriting, ad creatives, investment in brand and digital channels used.

It's definitely harder to move outside of the 'B2B guardrails', but the rewards for doing so when done right are massive.

#demandgeneration #b2bmarketingstrategy

👍❤️ 71   13 comments · 2 reposts

👍 Like   💬 Comment   ➝ Share   ✈ Send

I'm super passionate about this. In fact I used to get teased a bit because I'd say it so much. But I really do believe that B2B is still B2C. You're still marketing to people.

B2B marketing often falls into the trap of formal language, boring narratives and lifeless ads. But just because you're targeting a business, doesn't mean you have to be rigid. It's the people in those businesses making decisions - so target them.

Those people are still individuals. Getting the train, reading magazines, putting their kids to bed, popping to the pub for a drink. They're still people, with personalities, interests and goals.

There's no reason why we have to put ourselves into these formal confines when we communicate with our customers.

I felt we wanted to be different from a lot of the B2B companies I'd encountered before. I wanted us to be bold and fresh. I wanted to take some ideas that had been proven in B2C and try them in B2B.

Again, I want us to always be questioning 'are we doing things because we've always done them that way?' and 'is there a better way we could be doing things?'.

So remember that we're all humans. And we're just marketing to humans. So treat your B2B prospects like humans! And learn from B2C.

Building a media machine

 Alice De Courcy · 1st
Group Chief Marketing Officer at Cognism – Technical SaaS revenue...
1yr · 🌐

Coming off the back of a 2 day workshop with my London marketing team and we've made some big bets.

1️⃣ We are chucking away the rest of our H2 content calendar, giving our content writers creative freedom to 'go and find the story' in their specialisations. No more prescriptive planned titles on 'top tips for' or 'the ultimate guide to'

2️⃣ We are moving one of our content team away from writing and onto the problem of cracking 'content distribution'. We are aiming to build our own playbook for this to pave the way for 'creating once and distributing forever'.

We believe the combination of 1 & 2 together are going to elevate our marketing to the next level. Watch this space!

#demandgeneration # #contentstrategy

👍❤️ 90   2 comments

👍 Like   💬 Comment   → Share   ➤ Send

I love getting the whole team together to do some brainstorming. We come up with such great ideas when we have everyone bouncing off one another.

This was an H2 planning workshop where we made some choices for how we were going to work moving forwards.

One decision was to give our writers more creative freedom.

This was all a part of the switch away from traditional lead generation and moving to a demand generation first approach for our marketing.

You might wonder how these two things are related, the content writers aren't in the DG pods.

But what you have to remember is that the change from lead gen to demand gen doesn't just impact the DG team. It impacts all parts of the marketing function.

I knew that if we were to be successful in the switch, we needed to be creating game changingly good content in an already crowded space.

This is really difficult to do if you are planning out a content calendar months in advance.

You end up tied to titles and topics that have been assigned to you because months before, someone decided they'd be a good fit.

I wanted to turn it all on its head and create our own process.

If our content writers were able to be reactive to the trends and topics then we could take advantage of subjects getting traction in dark social. In other words, be talking about things our audience cares about, while they're still relevant.

The BBC or Reuters don't plan what they write months in advance. My hypothesis was that if we applied the same logic to B2B, our sales and marketing content could truly resonate and stand out.

If we wanted to be a true media machine and THE place that these professionals come to get their content insights, then we needed to act like journalists. So it was time to wave goodbye to the content calendar.

As someone who loves output, I was worried about ensuring that we still stay efficient from a content production standpoint.

Here you can look to set a 'story' number target and KPIs around traffic value or visitor growth that will hold the team accountable without the requirement for a content calendar.

One problem we have faced in the past is content distribution, so it's an area we have done a fair amount of experimentation in.

In the early days of our switch from lead gen to demand gen we had split out a content distributor as its own dedicated role sitting in the content team.

This got us some of the way there as it ensured that distribution had a focus, which helped in shifting the mindset.

But we found there was a big disconnect from the activities occurring in the demand generation team and that was an issue.

So we came up with an idea. To have dedicated DG Content Execs sitting in each of our DG pods.

It's important to note here that these content execs aren't just there to write blogs. They are content producers in all possible formats of content.

By sitting them in the demand gen pods, the distribution takes care of itself, as it is actioned via the DG activities and tactics.

So far this has been our unlock for building content distribution that can scale across channels and formats.

We have seen huge growth in our traffic numbers to our blog, the time spent on these blogs and ultimately the number of high intent demand demo requests that they drive.

We've also seen positive results such as:

→ High engagement within our 'always on' paid social campaigns.
→ Positive comments and shares of this content in dark social.

I fully believe this has been the key to building out a media machine of truly valuable content for our target audience. And that content can cut through the noise of a saturated market and ultimately plays a critical role in the whole demand generation strategy.

Redirection

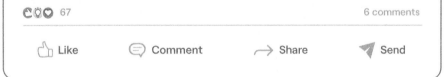

Alice De Courcy · 1st
Group Chief Marketing Officer at Cognism - Technical SaaS revenue...
1yr · 🌐

Lead generation and lead acquisition is not a problem for us.

Bold statement.

I know this to be true because we have a proven model we can dial up and down, our MDR's are consistently hitting and exceeding targets and our 'Inbound queue' is full to bursting.

But this isn't enough. It just buys us time.

We have given ourselves time to focus on the problem of generating higher levels of 'direct demand intent' and proving out a model that works here.

So we can be more creative with how we are generating this type of 'true demand and intent', and we are not tied to lead gen forms and gated content.

We had to earn the right to get here, and now we are here we need to prove out a predictable path to this new world before we can really leave the lead gen hamster wheel behind.

Start by delivering your numbers, then take incremental steps into a 'new way', back it with data and start to dial up what works while dialling down the 'old way'.

#demandgeneration #b2bmarketing #growthmarketing

😊👍❤️ 67   6 comments

👍 Like   💬 Comment   ➡️ Share   ✈️ Send

We earned the right to change direction.

But what happens after you've made the decision to make the switch?

Understand the task by getting your reporting in shape.

By splitting out my reporting into three clear funnels:

→ Direct intent demand demo requests.

→ MQLs (content leads).

→ And blended.

I was able to see the difference in efficiency between the direct declared intent and e-book MQLs.

I needed 25 demo requests to CW 1 deal vs 500 MQLs and MDR support to CW 1 MQL deal.

When you see this, the path forward becomes pretty clear. How can I fill my funnel with more demo requests? And if I do, I can cover the CW gap from MQLs quite easily.

I started to think:

How much would I pay to have my audience actually engage with and consume my content all the time, friction free, in the places they are already hanging out?

And would this consumption in our content result in a corresponding uplift in the number of people coming to the website and requesting to talk to us because they actually have intent to buy and have educated themselves?

At this stage we had cracked the code on generating MQLs, we could get an MQL for $10.

So I figured I could reduce our MQL campaigns down to just our highest performers, meaning those campaigns that could generate the most MQLs at the lowest cost.

Then, with the rest of the money, I redeployed it. Putting it into ungated, engagement first campaigns aimed at educating our prospects in-feed, friction free.

With this switch I wanted to see early indicators of success. For example, an increase in our direct demo requests month over month as we gradually ramped our create demand spend and reduced our MQL spend.
This is exactly what happened. Inbounds increased by 47%.

After three months of this approach, I was able to see the increase in direct inbounds producing the increased revenue needed to bridge the MQL gap.

Not only this, we were closing them faster, at a much better conversion rate and for higher ACVs.

If I was starting over today, I would start with this approach. I wouldn't go back to the lead gen model.

That is because I believe the way people want to buy and engage with B2B brands has changed. So the MQL playbook is unlikely to be effective for much longer.

Tales of an operational CMO

 Alice De Courcy · 1st

Group Chief Marketing Officer at Cognism - Technical SaaS revenue...

1yr · 🌐

Strategic CMO or operational?

This week I have been deep deep down in the nitty gritty.

I have been updating forms across sum 400+ landing pages for the deployment of lean data and faster inbound lead routing.

Getting reacquainted with Facebook Ads to build out our new demand funnels.

Creating new landing page templates for the un-gating and sunsetting of our content.

What have I learned from getting so close to the detail? I have come away with 10X more ideas for things we could start trying and do better. Some of those go live this week.

Sometimes it's the unglamorous work that has the biggest impact, and as a leader my philosophy is always to protect my team from any distractions and get it done. How do other people think about this?

#demandgeneration #growthmarketing #cmos

👏❤️ 79   16 comments · 1 repost

👍 Like   💬 Comment   ➡️ Share   ✈️ Send

I am an operational CMO and proud to be so.

How operational I am ebbs and flows depending on the business priorities at the time and on my capacity. But I will never stop being somewhat operational. And this is a great example of why:

Recently, we acquired a company called Kaspr. They operated a purely capture demand strategy to marketing. They had great CPLs because they were on relatively low spends, optimising campaigns for high-intent only.

Once they had joined the Cognism family, Kaspr's main goal was to start to scale, double budgets and double outputs.
Now we all know as marketers nothing is ever as simple as this. Especially if you are only running capture demand tactics.

At this stage I wasn't much involved in Kaspr's marketing. But after a couple of months of CPLs increasing, and significantly diminished returns, I got called in to have a look under the hood.

I mapped Kaspr's marketing sophistication out against that of the Cognism engine, a marketing engine that was successfully running both capture and create demand.

I built a roadmap for how we scale this sophistication from a 1 (just capture, no create demand, limited room to scale) to a 3 (both create and capture programmes running and optimised, with room to scale and stack growth).

But there was a problem.

Who would execute this?

We were hiring, but that would take months and we needed to get results fast.

I didn't want to distract my Cognism org and team with the tasks as they had their own targets to hit. So it fell to me to work alongside their marketer to get 'MVP create demand' activated and working.

If I was not operational, this would have been a two month blocker. And the growth would have stalled either with Kaspr or Cognism if I had distracted my team.

I know that would have been a big problem for my CEO and the board. And it would have cost the business revenue.

This is just one example and there have been many others, but this is why it quite literally pays to be an operational CMO.

Another example that springs to mind is this one.

While we were auditing and ungating our content during our move towards demand gen, I felt we hadn't properly thought through the aim and goal of the process.

What had been done:

→ Form removed from landing page.
→ PDF added in its place = ungating completed.

But after thinking about this process more deeply, this is what I came up with.

An interactive content page that could be easily consumed via sticky menus. Featuring helpful 'read more' content and videos added throughout the page. As well as personalised CTAs.

This may seem like a small tweak or adjustment, but the performance of these changes was massive.

In my post above I mention my philosophy around protecting my team from distractions to allow them to get work done.

This is critical in my view to being an effective CMO.

You need to be able to understand when and how to offload tasks in order to ensure your team can execute against the core strategy that will ultimately drive revenue.

If I am assigned a task that I think will be a distraction from the core revenue driving activity of the team, I will either:

1. Pushback.
2. Take it on myself.
3. Find it a new home.

In my early days at Cognism I did a lot of 1 and 2, as I wanted to prove my strategy and get my team executing.

As my time becomes more and more stretched, and with the aim to stay operational still front of mind. Now find that I do a lot more of 3.

The organisation is much more mature, and other departments have capacity and resources for more of these items.

But sometimes, like with the Kaspr example, a task just needs to get done and the best solution is to roll up your sleeves and execute yourself.

Finding this balance is not easy and it will shift as you scale and grow.

By building a team and culture that is focused on critical revenue generating tasks, you will find this becomes much easier to manage.

Buyers want instant gratification

 Alice De Courcy · 1st

Group Chief Marketing Officer at Cognism - Technical SaaS revenue...

1yr · 🌐

H2 is around the corner and we are changing things up!

It is much harder to build a predictable and repeatable marketing engine that doesn't rely on MQL's.

There is no 'playbook' for how this should look.

We won't change the machine overnight, but every week we are making tweaks to our tactics in the pursuit of a better way of doing B2B marketing.

It recognises the changes that have happened to how our buyers want to interact with us and how they want to buy.

Interested to hear what other marketing leaders are changing up for H2?

#b2bmarketing #demandmarketing #darkfunnel

🅲🅴♡ 36   5 comments

👍 Like   💬 Comment   ➡ Share   ✈ Send

The buying journey is not a linear one. Buyers do a lot more of their own research before reaching a purchase decision.

They go between review sites, and check out social media. They read emails, blogs and seek out peer recommendations. Overall, the buyer journey can be pretty unpredictable and untrackable.

This means they want information that allows them to make decisions on demand. Full access and instant gratification. So we ungated all our content.

They want content to be consumable in channel, zero click content - so we want to offer them value up front on channels like LinkedIn.

They want the option to engage with content in multiple formats. Such as written, audio and video - so we make sure ours covers these three content types.

The standard buyer's expectations have increased. Clickbait, high-level, written by a marketer with no subject matter expertise, doesn't cut it anymore. So we make sure each piece of content we produce is value-led, with actionable takeaways and has input from a subject matter expert.

Becoming a subject matter expert

Alice De Courcy · 1st

Group Chief Marketing Officer at Cognism - Technical SaaS revenue...

1yr · 🌐

· · ·

174% of Q2 revenue target + 58% of the quarters total revenue came from marketing.

A new record for the team!

A big part of how we are able to achieve these results is that we stay laser focused on our mission.

80/20 is the team philosophy.

I think this is so critical in marketing as you can so often get distracted with other tasks and 'busy work', but if they don't go to your core, or your north star, then you really have to scrutinise why you are doing them.

A company wide agreement and senior stakeholder buy in is vital if this is going to work.

#demandmarketing #b2bmarketing

🅒🅒♡ 36   5 comments

👍 Like   💬 Comment   → Share   ✈ Send

You may have noticed I've started filming a lot more video and using the content for my LinkedIn posts.

I realised there was an added benefit from turning myself into a subject matter expert for our marketing audience. I could repurpose the video I was making.

That's advice I'd give anyone in my position, don't be afraid to use content more than once.

Many people won't see it the first time. And assuming it still holds true and is valuable, re-using that content is making it work harder for you. It also increases the chances of your target audience consuming it.

I was already filming video as part of my subject matter expert work within the Cognism media machine. It's a a key part of our create demand strategy.

So because I could repurpose this video, it wasn't any more effort for me versus my written posts.

It actually made posting much easier as I had a springboard for post ideas. No more starting with a blank piece of paper!

I could pick parts of conversations I had already had in webinars that I knew had been of interest to the live attendees, and build on these.

I didn't notice any crazy changes in engagement on LinkedIn but I know myself as a user that it just diversifies how people can consume the content.

Many people will watch a video and not comment or like. And by supporting a text post with video, I was able to get more people to consume the content which is exactly what we are after at the end of the day.

Going back to the post above itself, I wanted to go into more detail on what I mean by the 80/20 rule.

Marketing, arguably more than any other department, needs strict guardrails when it comes to how it supports the rest of the organisation. These guardrails are also helpful for how marketing prioritises its own work.

You could spend 100% of your time on 'busy work' that won't actually move the needle in terms of achieving your core business goals or driving marketing revenue.

When I joined Cognism, marketing was 100% 'busy work' and sales enablement. It was not proactive in any way. Ultimately this led to unpredictable and limited revenue contributions and effectiveness.

In order to create real impact and change, you need to show leadership and executives a roadmap for hitting the business objectives and get this signed off upfront.

This then becomes your key mechanism for pushing back on tasks that don't impact directly on your end goal.

You should still leave yourself and your team with some capacity. Around 20%. This can be used for unplanned but critical items that will inevitably crop up.

I also find that working in bi-weekly sprints helps to keep focus. It ensures that the majority of your team's time and effort is going into the activities and initiatives that will make an impact on your agreed business objectives.

As your org grows, you may find it harder to minimise the distractions from outside of marketing. But coming together for these bi-weekly sprints will provide visibility and enable the correct re-prioritisation and focus.

Setting records

Alice De Courcy · 1st

Group Chief Marketing Officer at Cognism - Technical SaaS revenue...

3yr · 🌐

···

Best ever, record revenue setting month for marketing...August 21!

We ended the month 190% of revenue target and contributing over 75% of the NB revenue number for the month. We typically do 53%.

So how did we do this?

I've been documenting a lot on here about our journey from a lead gen model to a demand focused one, and I believe that August, as shown on the below graph, is the first sign of the compounding results/impact that all of these new shifts can have on revenue performance.

Key changes we have made/are making to drive this performance & uptick in direct inbounds and resulting revenue:

1. Shift focus and spend away from gated content and generating MQL's. Instead focus on engaging the market with content vs collecting email addresses from it.

2. Turn up, repeatedly, in the channels that your b2b buyers are using to make decisions and engage with content: Podcasts, Communities, Organic & Paid LinkedIn, Paid FB & Instagram, YouTube.

3. Give content distribution the focus it needs-we now have someone on this full-time.

4. Raise your content game by utilising subject matter experts. Write content for engagement and memorability vs pure SEO rank and clickbait.

#demandmarketing #b2bmarketing #marketingleadership

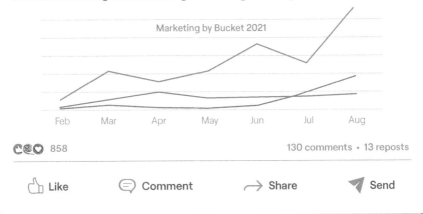

Marketing by Bucket 2021

Feb   Mar   Apr   May   Jun   Jul   Aug

😀😍👍 858   130 comments · 13 reposts

👍 Like   💬 Comment   ➜ Share   ✈ Send

This was a big moment.

It was the point at which it was clear to me that we had successfully made the switch from lead generation to demand generation.

Some of the key changes we had made at this stage were:

→ **Content that added real value to our audience.** We delivered this by utilising and investing in subject matter experts to contribute to our content. We also ditched the pre-planned content calendar and shifted our focus to topics that were trending at the time.

→ **Content optimised for consumption in the channel it was delivered.** We shifted away from trying to force actions on our audience and instead doubled down on producing content that could be consumed natively, with minimum friction. Optimising for consumption, rather than clicks and conversions.

→ **Balancing delivery of thought leadership content with content about our product.** It can be tempting when you pivot away from lead generation to over-index on thought leadership content and forget about building out and delivering your product content in the same ways. We spent a lot of time focusing on building out persona-focused product content. This included things like workflow product tours, specific case study use cases talked to and shown by our customer success reps, FAQs, objection handling videos and more.

→ **We thoughtfully ungated our content.** Creating long-form assets from the best of our gated content, building out resources and website journeys that drove engagement and consumption of this content.

→ **We found the channels on which our target audience spent time.** We paid to distribute this content on them, optimising for in-feed consumption and engagement.

These are just some of the notable changes we had made at this stage that had started to compound and drive these impressive results.

ABM or ABhmmmm

Alice De Courcy · 1st

Group Chief Marketing Officer at Cognism - Technical SaaS revenue...

1yr · 🌐

Current thinking on ABM...caution could be controversial!

Successful ABM is not...

- Buying an expensive piece of technology to serve my target accounts with display ads on platforms that they don't actually spend time on, or very little time on

- Building an overcomplicated programme aimed at pushing my target accounts through a funnel that they are not ready for

Successful ABM is...

- Deeply understanding what differentiates your key buyers in those target accounts, where they engage with content, and what problems they have right now
- Providing that content in engaging formats in the channels that these buyers are in and in which they will spend time on: queue dark social
- Consistently adding a level of value in both the above that ensures your are both creating AND accelerating demand in these accounts

I would rather spend money on content experts, consistent distribution within dark social channels and a podcast of the quality that key buyers in my accounts will listen to for 20-30 minutes, every week, over a piece of tech that MAY capture an impression or two and I can claim influenced opportunity on.

#b2bmarketing #demandmarketing #accountbasedmarketing

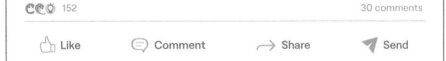

💬😊👏 152   30 comments

👍 Like   💬 Comment   ➡ Share   ✈ Send

Account Based Marketing. Another overused and often misunderstood term in B2B marketing.

The worst offenders (in my view) are those that think 'we must do ABM' and then go and buy an expensive piece of software to effectively run ABM programmes, only to be disappointed.

Ultimately no tech can solve the larger issues at play:

→ Spending time building and refining a proper target list of accounts and contacts. This is an ongoing piece of work and is the most critical step.

→ Understanding what it is that these contacts care about and where they are hanging out to get the answers to these questions. I expect that the reality is that your programmatic display 'air cover' ads are not hitting your contacts with either the right content or in the right places.

→ The best ABM motions I've seen have been run using Google Sheets or a project management tool to track the execution of highly personalised manual tasks that no ABM platform has the power to enable.

→ ABM does not have to be overly complicated. It is just a more personalised and targeted experience of your demand gen plays. At the core of it all is truly valuable content, delivered in the places and formats that they want to engage with.

We don't run ABM at Cognism because we don't need to. But if I did run ABM, I would build an MVP programme, track and run it on Google Sheets and validate the success before I even think about taking on tech to scale it out.

Know your audience

 Alice De Courcy · 1st

Group Chief Marketing Officer at Cognism – Technical SaaS revenue...

1yr · 🌐

The greatest thing you can do as a marketer is talk to your customers and prospects.

I'm in a fortunate position that my peers are also very often my customers and prospects and so running our podcast, Revenue Champions, doubles as a formidable content asset, and also a huge customer insight activity.

Yesterday I spoke to Doug Bell, the new CMO at LeanData and long time career CMO.

Doug gave some practical tips on getting your first marketing leadership role and how to tackle you first 30, 60 and 90 days when you do.

He also spilled his take on the demand gen marketing movement.

Link in comments to Revenue Champions, give it a follow to be notified when this one goes live.

#b2bmarketing #demandgeneration #marketingleadership

 65   7 comments

👍 Like   💬 Comment   ➴ Share   ✈ Send

When you make the move to demand generation, you can't take shortcuts when it comes to understanding your customer and prospects.

The success of your demand generation execution will rely on this knowledge. So you can produce valuable content at scale in the places that they want to engage with it.

We speak to our prospects and customers daily as part of our media machine and content production process.

Whether that be in an interview for a blog, a podcast episode or a live event.

I will always try and take five minutes to ask these people:

→ What content are they enjoying right now?
→ What do they wish there was more of?
→ How they like to do their learning.
→ In what format?
→ And on which channels?

The truth is, people don't mind answering these questions and the insights are huge.

So next time you have time with a prospect or customer, make sure you take the opportunity to ask these research questions.

Top tip:

Have a process for feeding back these insights to the team. Otherwise they may well exist in a silo, and you won't reap the benefits.

Looking for unicorns

Alice De Courcy · 1st

Group Chief Marketing Officer at Cognism - Technical SaaS revenue...

1yr · 🌐

Another huge quarter delivered by the amazing Cognism marketing team. 129% of an increased NB revenue target 🚀.

No looking back on our pivot from a lead generation approach to demand generation focus.

AND thanks to all this amazing growth we are hiring!

I am looking for 3 new revenue focused marketers to join us in setting the standard for B2B Marketing.

Open roles are:

Senior SEO & Content Executive - we are looking for someone who can take a strategic approach to SEO and an editorial focus to content writing - https://lnkd.in/dtYU5ndt

Paid Media Marketing Manager - we are looking for someone to come and work on all our 'capture demand' work - https://lnkd.in/dBqKBAGd

DACH Senior Campaign Marketer - we are expanding rapidly in the DACH region and need another revenue focused DACH marketer to speed up this acceleration - https://lnkd.in/dz54wE3R

And please no recruiters - we have this covered :)

#demandgeneration #b2bmarketing

 125   12 comments · 1 repost

👍 Like   💬 Comment   ➡ Share   ✈ Send

The best thing about making the pivot from lead gen to demand gen?

We earned the right to scale.

I'm always cautious about hiring. My philosophy is that each role should be maxed out in capacity before we look to bring on a new hire.

It's been game-changing to be able to prove the repeatable scaling success of the marketing engine and get the buy-in for growing the team.

When your CEO says: 'this is great, how can we do more and scale faster?' That is any marketing leader's dream.

Remember, the answer will often not be to chuck more money at capturing demand by increasing spend on Google Ads. It's likely to lie in stacking growth through your create demand activities, and these will require more people power.

So why was I hiring for these roles specifically?

Well, we had proved the positive impact that SEO could have on generating revenue more efficiently.

We had built out and scaled our SEO efforts, despite having limited resources or internal dedicated expertise.

It was at this stage that it made sense to invest in an internal SEO expert who could take ownership of continuing to scale our SEO efforts and give it independent focus.

SEO had proven its place in our repeatable marketing revenue engine and capacity had been hit, so it was time to hire.

Next, onto the Paid Media Marketing Manager. Boy, I have had a journey with this role!

So hopefully I can help stop you making all the same mistakes that I've made.

Firstly, DO NOT outsource this position if you are only going to spend a small amount of money with the agency you outsource it to.

Why?

You get what you pay for.

An agency is only going to be able to deliver to a limited extent.
They will optimise for in-platform metrics, but they will not be optimising for revenue.

They will also not be in a position to pull important levers on landing page messaging and content that can be crucial to how your campaigns perform.

Another important lesson I learned is that you need this role to be critical in your:

→ Budgeting pacing, tracking and adjusting

→ Paid reporting, forecasting and planning

An agency is very unlikely to be able to do any of this as well as someone who sits in the org.

BUT the cost of hiring a bad paid marketing person is big. So make sure you run a case study interview process.

I would want to be sure that this person can own:

→ Budget pacing.

→ Can run a spend forecast.

→ Look after the re-planning process.

→ Can optimise campaigns for revenue and not platform metrics.

→ Finally, I'd want them to understand the difference between creating demand and capturing it, and that they are across the metrics and strategies behind both of these.

Eventually, we found our unicorn in this role. But it took us a year and a half of pain to get there.

My advice would be:

Don't compromise or rush the hire.

It's much better to fill the gap with a freelancer until you have found your unicorn.

This can be a game-changing role, for better or worse, depending on your success in hiring the right person.

Finally, we hired our DACH marketer because we had proven the success of our marketing strategy in this new region and we were ready to start to scale revenue there.

A proud CMO moment

 Alice De Courcy · 1st

Group Chief Marketing Officer at Cognism – Technical SaaS revenue...

1yr · 🌐

Interested in seeing inside the marketing engine that has been powering over half of the new business revenue growth at Cognism?

Cognism's marketing team are out in force today and tomorrow at the B2B Marketing Expo. Incredibly proud of all of them, some amazing talks, hugely actionable and a good look inside the Cognism marketing strategy.

Masterclasses running all day today and tomorrow next to our stand.

Fran Langham, Liam Bartholomew Joe Barron Oscar Frost Greig Kaj Robertson James Sutton and Richard Tank

#b2bmarketing21 #b2bmarketing #demandgeneration

👍❤️ 90   2 comments

 Like   Comment   → Share   ✈ Send

This was definitely a highlight of 2021 for me.

It was a real 'stop and look how far you have come' moment.

And this wasn't anything to do with my talk at the B2B Expo. It was seeing my amazing team in action - sharing all of their learnings in front of 100s of fellow marketers.

I promise, I'm not just saying this because I'm biased - but they all stood out. They were delivering inspiring, actionable content, setting the standard for B2B marketing in the UK.

We were addressing marketing tactics and execution that most people had not been able to start doing yet which was huge!

All the strategy, planning and execution in the world won't get you very far as a team of one.

You have to build a team that will take the foundations and run with them.

I've found much more success hiring people who might be a little less experienced with marketing, but fundamentally understand the shift we are making in our demand gen first philosophy. We can teach them the execution skills much more easily than the mindset.

A CMOs superpower has to be hiring. It's so critical.

So this was a great time for me to take stock of my incredible team of demand first marketers.

I watched in awe at how easily they took on the challenge of speaking at this event and sharing all of their knowledge and insights.

Making predictions

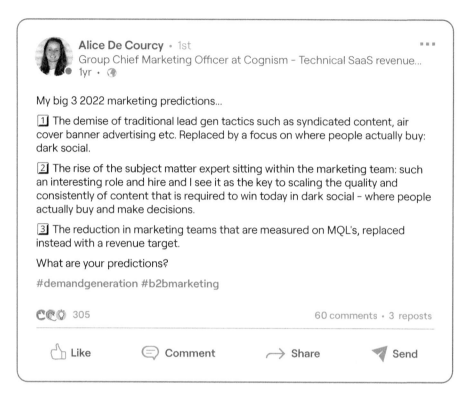

> **Alice De Courcy** · 1st
> Group Chief Marketing Officer at Cognism - Technical SaaS revenue...
> 1yr · 🌐
>
> My big 3 2022 marketing predictions...
>
> 1️⃣ The demise of traditional lead gen tactics such as syndicated content, air cover banner advertising etc. Replaced by a focus on where people actually buy: dark social.
>
> 2️⃣ The rise of the subject matter expert sitting within the marketing team: such an interesting role and hire and I see it as the key to scaling the quality and consistently of content that is required to win today in dark social - where people actually buy and make decisions.
>
> 3️⃣ The reduction in marketing teams that are measured on MQL's, replaced instead with a revenue target.
>
> What are your predictions?
>
> #demandgeneration #b2bmarketing
>
> 👍❤️💡 305   60 comments · 3 reposts
>
> 👍 Like   💬 Comment   ➡️ Share   ✈️ Send

It's so interesting to look back at this and see how far we have come with the three points I mention in this post. It's a little mind-boggling how much the industry as a whole has changed in this time as well.

My take today (October 2022), all three of these are happening, but only in organisations with forward-thinking marketers.

I believe there's still an opportunity for other marketers to embrace these ideas. In fact, I feel that soon, they'll become as normal as gated e-books were two years ago.

For us at Cognism specifically, we have fully embraced all three of these and it has enabled us to deliver record revenue and pipeline quarters throughout the year.

We don't run any lead generation plays anymore. We focus only on capturing existing high-intent demand and creating demand in order to drive more high intent demo requests.

The results?

Our high-intent demo requests have increased month-on-month, proving the success of the shift away from MQLs.

We can now confidently say we don't miss MQLs in our marketing mix.

We now use all the time and spend from MQLs and direct it towards creating demand initiatives. That has proven to be game-changing for us. It's far more scalable.

The second prediction - the rise of subject matter experts. This has been a huge part of how we have shifted time and spend in new ways since departing from running lead generation.

So let's take a look at what we have done here at Cognism.

We've now taken on multiple subject matter experts across our two core persona's (sales and marketing) and been working with them consistently across 2022.

Sales SME's:

1. **David Bentham.** Dave is Director, Sales Development @ Cognism.
2. **Morgan J. Ingram.** Morgan is a renowned Sales Development expert.
3. **Ryan Reisert.** Ryan is another renowned Cold Calling expert and also founder of Phone Ready Leads.

Our marketing SME's:

1. Myself, **Alice de Courcy**, CMO @ Cognism
2. **Liam Bartholomew**, Global Head of Demand Generation @ Cognism
3. **Fran Langham**, Head of Demand Generation @ Cognism
4. **Gaetano DiNardi,** Growth Advisor and fractional VP

So what have we been doing with these SMEs?

We have been committing to consistent high quality content output week in, week out, in multiple formats:

→ Live cold calling trainings.
→ Short top tip videos for SDRs.
→ Weekly interviews for new topics for our blog and sales newsletter.
→ TikToks.
→ Development of their own personal LinkedIn organic channel through consistent posting (Dave Bentham).

So, what sort of results has this work been driving?

1. Dark social engagement

We have so many examples of SDRs posting or messaging our SMEs to thank them for their helpful content.

We repurpose this content for the Cognism company page. And we've seen a record year for growth in followers and engagement.

Finally, we have seen our SMEs being listed on our human attribution form on our demo thank-you page. Prospects credit them as the reason for requesting a demo of Cognism.

2. Paid social performance

We now run a fully ungated and engagement focused paid social strategy, our priority is quality and valuable content.

We have to consistently produce this type of content in a repeatable and sustainable manner. Having SMEs to drive this has been the key for being able to do so.

3. Blog engagement

The posts we write based on our SME content and insights are nearly always those that deliver benchmark beating stats in terms of time on page (5-6 mins) and views.

We are building a media machine that will see Cognism as THE go-to resource for content that will actually help you if you are a B2B sales or marketing professional. SME content and insights are a critical part of enabling us to deliver that.

4. Owned channel growth

Whether it's:

→ Website traffic.
→ YouTube subscribers.
→ LinkedIn followers.
→ Podcast listeners.
→ Or newsletter subscribers.

Our SMEs have enabled us to build an audience of loyal listeners and readers.

Random acts of marketing

 Alice De Courcy · 1st

Group Chief Marketing Officer at Cognism – Technical SaaS revenue...

1yr · 🌐   ● ● ●

Great marketing, marketing that gets you to your revenue number month after month, is about committing to a path and executing it very well or better than others. Again and again.

In 2022 I won't be focusing on 'the next big thing', or running away from some of the well trodden marketing tactics that are being touted as 'dead' today: SEO, Event Marketing, even Gated Content.

All of these things can have a place in your marketing strategy, you just need to spend the time to work out how you can do them better than others and how you should be pivoting your approach to them.

One thing that is sure always to fail is mediocre marketing, and that for sure, is dead.

#demandgeneration #marketingstrategy #b2bmarketing

 157   13 comments · 2 reposts

👍 Like   💬 Comment   ↗ Share   ✈ Send

Execution.

I've touched on this quite a lot throughout this diary and my LinkedIn posts. But I think it's fair to say execution is critical to be successful.

Refine Labs introduced me to the term 'random acts of marketing'. And that summarises what I was trying to hit on in this post. More importantly, it was what I wanted to avoid doing in 2022.

I think this becomes even more important as your team grows, more people does not always mean more output, if you don't have the right focus and processes in place.

So how do you create an environment where people execute? And importantly, execute meaningfully rather than randomly?

The starting point as a leader is being very clear on what metrics matter, and where you are placing your bets to drive forward those metrics.

You need to think about this like a campaign. You need to repeat the message over and over again. And you need to have regular cadences for stopping, reviewing and refocusing.

For us, that looks like bi-weekly sprint cycles and running all of our tasks through a project management tool - Asana.

If it's not on Asana - it didn't happen.

Sprints enable us to be reactive to shifting priorities based on insights and how we are tracking towards our core metrics. Many campaigns and ideas have met their early demise through this methodology. And it's really helped us to keep scaling output with headcount effectively.

When I interview, I always set a practical case study. This is because I value execution so much. I have worked with 'ideas' people before, and ultimately their impact is very limited. Mostly because they are unable to transition from ideation to action.

In every role I have held, my bias to action has always been the thing that gets highlighted above all else as being my critical strength.

This coupled with a mindset of, 'done is better than perfect', are core traits that I believe you need if you are going to be effective in marketing. Start practising these traits daily, and the incremental impact will be surprising.

Sourcing subject matter experts

Alice De Courcy · 1st

Group Chief Marketing Officer at Cognism – Technical SaaS revenue...

1yr · 🌐

Have you thought about hiring a subject matter expert into your marketing team?

It was top of my 2022 'to do' list here at Cognism.

Making the decision to hire was the easy bit, but finding the right person for the job was much harder.

So I'm very excited to announce that we'll be partnering with Ryan Reisert in 22, to see what impact we can have by combining his subject matter expertise with our marketing engine!

I'll make sure to document our journey and learnings as we go.

#demandmarketing #demandgeneration #b2bmarketing

🫶👏❤️ 71   10 comments

👍 Like   💬 Comment   ➡ Share   ✈ Send

Subject matter experts. I touched on this earlier on, but what I didn't talk about is how to go about hiring or finding people to work with.

On the marketing side, this was relatively easy for us because we could lean on our internal expertise.

When it came to sales, it was more difficult.

At the start, there was a certain level of scepticism internally. Especially within the sales org in relation to how valuable this could be. Was it really worth any internal sales experts giving up time for this type of activity?

This led me to look externally for someone I could work with to prove the impact of the role.

Now it is vital when you're looking for an SME that you find someone who is still doing the work they talk about.

Why?

Because it means they are still learning, and they will have a consistent flow of insights to bring to the content they produce with you.

Be realistic in your search. You're likely to have budget constraints. So you're not necessarily going to be able to work with a Top 10 influencer in your space right away.

Try and find that sweet spot. Choose someone who already engages with your audience's community on a regular basis. But they don't have to have hit full influencer status yet.

We found our perfect match with Ryan Reisert here.

Ryan loved cold calling, and he still does. And he is doing the job daily, making his insights so valuable.

He was equally bought into the idea of being an SME and the business impact this could have. So he was very committed. This is very important as consistency is what will truly drive success.

Set clear KPIs for what you want to achieve with your SME. Here are the KPIs that I set with Ryan:

Goal / KPI

Scale LinkedIn followers to over 24K by the end of June 22. Adding 1K a month.

Contributing to an uplift in organic unique blog views of 25% every quarter.

Become the voice of the sales newsletter, with subscribers increased by 50% every quarter.

Become the host of the Revenue Champions Podcast, sourcing influential and interesting speakers on a weekly basis and helping to scale regular active listeners to 150, from 35. Host an episode every week.

Produce regular video content to help drive YouTube subscribers up & to keep our 'always on' sales content paid social buckets performing above benchmarks.

Run regular live events. Minimum of one every other week.

We managed to achieve or exceed each of these KPIs! And we got such great feedback on Ryan's content too:

Miriam Owusu
Helping SMEs Find, Bid and Win Public Sector Tenders

Hello Ryan,

Miriam from London.

Great presentation on cold-calling!

Appreciate the gems of advice!

Brian Fischer
Director of Business Development/Sales at Regroup Mass Notification

Ryan love what your doing. Your content is above the rest by far for cold calling on LinkedIn.

Keep it up, love to make some live calls some day with you.

Been at it for 11 years, never have I wrote somebody on their content before.

More in sales need to believe in what your doing!

Rethinking funding press releases

Alice De Courcy · 1st

Group Chief Marketing Officer at Cognism - Technical SaaS revenue...

1yr · 🌐

Funding press releases...love or hate them? https://lnkd.in/etg-mZhP

For me it is a great opportunity to stand back and take stock of how far we've come and look ahead to a very exciting future.

2021 saw the Cognism marketing achieve 130% of our revenue target - which is 53% of the total new business number, so that's pretty phenomenal.

In 2021 we hit some key milestones as a marketing team:

- Moving from a lead gen to a demand gen approach and successfully predictably scaling our direct inbound channel
- Creating a working framework and process for approaching content distribution
- Achieving a monthly organic traffic value of over $104K
- Significantly growing our owned subscriber channels: newsletters, YouTube and our Podcast
- Building a repeatable, scalable Enterprise marketing approach
- Hiring, retaining & promoting some amazing marketing talent

This was all powered by an incredible team: Vera Kalinn (Verche Karafiloska), Liam Bartholomew, Karin O'Grady, Fran Langham, Richard Tank, Joe Barron, James Sutton, Emma Sexton, Emma Sands, Ilse V Rensburg, Di Frost, Oscar Frost, Greig Kaj Robertson, Binal Raval, Emily Liu, Ognen Bojkovski, Nicole Peters, Ashleigh Frank, and Stevco Naumoski

🅒🅒♡ 85   14 comments · 1 repost

👍 Like   💬 Comment   ➡ Share   ✈ Send

Funding press releases get a lot of hate.

And I agree that they are not news. Sometimes they can be relied upon as lazy marketing execution in order to generate some short-lived noise.

Now, this is only true if you approach them in the way that they have always been done.

Write a press release and send it out to journalists. Then pray that it gets picked up by TechCrunch and reshare the 'news' on your blog and socials.

But you can use it to spearhead some creative marketing execution that can actually have an impact.

Why not hold a live press conference on the funding announcement, getting your CEO to answer audience questions live?

You can use it to look back on all the things that drove the growth that led to this success. By that, I mean the tactical pieces of the engine that made an impact.

So next time you have a funding announcement, think about how you can take that and use it to spearhead some creative marketing around it.

Kissing frogs

Alice De Courcy · 1st
Group Chief Marketing Officer at Cognism - Technical SaaS revenue...
1yr · 🌐

I have been kissing a LOT of frogs recently 🐸!

Some of these were playstation playing gamer frogs

Some were yawning, swearing frogs

Some were just generally uninterested and unimpressed frogs

Don't worry, this is not a love story, I haven't found a prince, but I have found some unicorn marketers!

I've been busy getting stuck back into a lot of screening/first round interviews and I have learnt a lot by doing so.

It can be painful, it can be a big suck on your time, but the excitement of uncovering exceptional talent is worth it all.

How many marketing leaders do screening calls and first round interviews? Should we be doing them more often?

I think being able to hire well is SO important when you are a marketing leader, and to be good at it, you need to hone your skills and do LOTS of it.

Top tips to all marketers interviewing right now:

1. Please don't plat playstation on the interview - we love to see multi-tasking, but this is one step too far!

2. Please don't complain about the time of the interview, it is a two way thing and everyone on that call has given up their time to be there.

3. Enthusiasm, passion, research and listening can go a long way.

Here's to kissing more frogs in 2022!

#b2bmarketing #marketinghiring

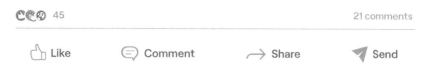

🔵💬👍 45   21 comments

👍 Like   💬 Comment   → Share   ✈ Send

Hiring. It should be a CMO superpower. Especially in the early days when you're building out your team. Your hires can make-or-break your productivity.

Hiring and onboarding can feel like a big distraction at the time. But it is one of the things that you can do which will have the largest impact, negatively or positively. Depending on how successful you are at it.

You can also learn so much about the types of people you're attracting to the role, meaning you learn about how to write or alter job specs.

I'd never want to give up the chance to filter in or out the right candidates. Although, I'll admit it does change when you scale. We have made about 15 hires this year and I certainly haven't been around for all of the first round interviews.

Sometimes I need to assess how critical the role is against my other time requirements.

But I have put some rules in place:

1. I will always be present for the final stage interviews, no matter the role.
2. Everyone involved in the hire agrees on the candidate. If one person on the interview panel says no, then it's a no.

Using these two foundational principles, we have had great success in our recruitment efforts.

And yes... if you're wondering, the story about the guy playing PlayStation during his interview is true.

That's not even the whole story. He had told us he was out of work at the time, so interviewing for a new role was his full-time job. And yet he complained about the time of his interview!

Admittedly, it was 5:30pm on a Friday - so not exactly a prime time slot.

However, we had been very busy that week, and this was a critical role we were hiring for. I was keen to be involved in the process - so we booked the interview for a time when I could attend.

Unfortunately, it was clear that he had done no research into who each of the people on the interview panel were. And it was a little jarring to hear a candidate be so openly vocal about the interview time. Only to waste his shot by playing PlayStation throughout.

That's one downside to a CMO being so involved in first stage interviews... Sometimes you come across some time-wasters.
But some good news. We finally filled the role we were struggling to fill the most, Head of Paid Performance - with a unicorn marketer!

My advice to anyone struggling to fill a role like this? Don't rush it. Ignore the pressure to fill it fast with the wrong person. Panic-hiring is the worst thing you can do.

Instead:

→ Set yourself standards for what you're looking for in a marketer and stick to them.
→ Stay patient.
→ Find creative ways to fill the role in the interim. For example we used a freelancer to fill the gap before we hired our unicorn!
→ Be creative in the ways in which you attract your candidates.

That last point is an important one, as we found a way to attract talent who have a similar mindset and already buy into our way of thinking.

How?

Through our online marketing event series, Demandism.

We've essentially built an entire community and following, with around 100 regular listeners based around our shift to demand generation.

And we've made three hires, including the recent Head of Paid Performance, who came inbound to us after listening to Demandism.

In other words, we created and advertised our culture for demand-first marketing, which encouraged others who share the same philosophy to want to come and work for us.

And each of them said during the interview process that they wanted to work for Cognism because they felt they could learn and grow more in this forward-thinking company versus anywhere else.

They were already sold on the job before they got to the interview, which is great for us.

We have received some brilliant cover letters, I'll leave you an example below:

Dear hiring manager,

My name's Jamie. I'm a B2B marketer based in London, with four years of experience devising and executing integrated marketing campaigns across property, B2B events, sports media and consulting.

I would be thrilled to be considered for the open position at Cognism.

Full disclosure – I'm an avid follower of Refine Labs, Chris Walker, Dave Gerhardt, Full Funnel and others that are speaking the language I believe is the future of

B2B marketing. Revenue focused, demand-driven, buyer-centric marketing.

Cognism instantly stood out to me as a UK based voice passionate about this shift. I share that passion and believe this, coupled with my track record of impact in previous roles, make me a great fit for the role.

Some achievements from my previous employment include:

→ Increasing attendance for SportsPro Insider Series brand by 23% from October 2020 – May 2021

→ Led on email marketing campaigns for SportsPro Insider Series averaging 58% open rate & 5.56% click rate from October 2020 – May 2021

→ Led on email marketing campaigns for BlackBook Motorsport averaging 50% open rate & 5.46% click rate from October 2020 – May 2021

→ Responsible for SportsPro's first ROI positive Google Ads campaign with 4421% ROAS

→ Oversaw multiple LinkedIn retargeting campaigns averaging 56% conversion rate

→ Promoted to Marketing Manager in May 2021

Overall, I would offer proven copywriting skills, extensive experience managing organic and paid social channels, experience driving revenue with email marketing as well as demonstrable experience in PPC, SEO and content marketing.

I also believe I offer a good cultural fit for the role.

What do I believe about marketing and where it's heading?

Marketing must be led with first-hand customer insights, these qualitative indicators drive strategy

→ The lead gen model is outdated. Running direct response ads and passing low intent leads to sales isn't buyer-centric and is based on flawed thinking

→ The future of marketing lies in shifting focus to activities and channels that drive demand and stimulate word of mouth

→ B2B marketers must recognise that 95% of potential buyers are not in-market, these prospects need to be educated and nurtured with content in the places where they actually spend time

Outside of that, I also genuinely love what I do – and hope I've conveyed that in this letter. I would be delighted to discuss my application further in person and hope to hear back from you.

Kind regards,

Jamie Skeels

Hands-on mode

Alice De Courcy · 1st

Group Chief Marketing Officer at Cognism - Technical SaaS revenue...

1yr · 🌐

•••

As a marketing leader you can get carried away with strategic work, but some times the key is in the details...

It's vital, and can actually drive pretty critical results.

Some of the areas that have been getting my attention recently:

- UTM tracking set-up: are we getting valuable AND actionable data from these, what role does it play in our strategy and decision making?

- Organic LinkedIn posting strategy review. Is our channel living up to it's purpose: a place where our audience can find tips, tactics and insights that will make their work day better - all in feed. Finding: too much us and not enough them

- Technical SEO. This one is definitely unglamorous work. I am getting pretty familiar with every URL and redirect across our 400+ pages and counting!

- BOFU paid ads execution. This one has been very valuable, a combination of changing the way we work and looking at new ways to execute.

Big picture strategy stuff is certainly important, but if the rest doesn't follow then what is the point of that strategic deck collecting dust in the corner.

I view all of these pieces as the building blocks to stacking our growth and enabling us to hit those revenue goals.

#demandgeneration

🔵⚫♡ 88   8 comments

👍 Like   💬 Comment   ➔ Share   ✈ Send

You can see throughout my posts when I go from 'strategic mode' into 'hands-on mode'.

This is one example of when I've decided to get into the nitty gritty – and you can see there were four main areas I wanted to look at.

1. UTM tracking set-up

Tracking a demand generation strategy is difficult. It's not always possible to directly attribute what has been successful.

Unfortunately, there are a lot of insights that you lose when you don't gate content anymore.

Yes, we knew that what we were doing was working. After all, we were hitting targets and generating revenue and pipeline at record rates.

But if we were being held to account for the exact initiative that was having the biggest impact. That would have been quite difficult to say.

So you need other ways to measure the activities you're doing and the impact on pipeline and revenue.

We went back to the drawing board in terms of how we set up our UTMs.

And this task was one of those times when I just had to roll up my sleeves, assess how the process would work with our marketing operations team and implement it throughout the org.

2. Organic LinkedIn posting strategy review

For a while, we had fallen into a trap of posting thoughtlessly on LinkedIn. We chose to put out things like case studies or links to new content. Without really considering what people would like to see.

I wanted to bring back a lens, looking at LinkedIn as a channel to showcase the value we offer upfront.

So I worked with the marketer who was looking after the LinkedIn channel at the time and drew a line in the sand. No more promotional content. At all. None. Everything has to be value-based.

Going back to basics really helped us to keep true to our mission.

It took a few weeks for everyone to settle into this idea. For example, the DG team would ask to share a case study on the LinkedIn page. I'd step in and say no, we should run that as part of our paid 'always on' social-proof bucket. That's not for organic LinkedIn.

But after the first two or three weeks, we were back to being completely value-focused. And our LinkedIn has gone from strength-to-strength since then.

In fact, our follower growth has increased by 84% more between January and November this year in comparison to March to December last year. And our engagement is up 46.7% in the same time period.

3. Technical SEO

Up until not too long ago, we didn't have any SEO expertise in-house. Myself and the Senior Content Manager just handled it ourselves with the self-taught knowledge we had.

So we have definitely had a technical SEO gap and generally, what we did do was what I was able to do myself. Yes, not the most glamorous tasks but I didn't want to hand off the responsibility to anyone else in-house when we didn't yet have the required expertise.

Eventually it got to a stage when I realised that the amount of work that needed to be done to keep our health score up, alongside all the other SEO-related work we could be doing didn't scale.

We needed to bring in resources to cover these tasks so I could be freed up in other areas.

4. BOFU ad execution

This has been one of the biggest reasons for our success in demand generation.

Something I don't think we truly understood when we pivoted away from lead gen was that we needed to over-index on all of the bottom of funnel content that we created. In addition, we needed to think carefully about how we distributed that.

Because you will fail if all you look at is content and thought leadership.

Yes, you'll be adding value to your audience - but you also won't be educating them at all on your product.

We needed to build out this bucket. We didn't really have any supporting assets for this, and yes, we could spin up some ads on Cognism's quality data and blah blah blah.

But where would the ad go to? What would the page look like? How would we make it somewhere that our audience would spend time? Did we have videos explaining how our product operates? What would the workflow be?

One of our key learnings from testing the above approaches is 'be human'. Don't shy away from promoting a video just because it has a tiny mistake in it.

Done is better than perfect and nine times out of ten your audience will prefer the more raw version.

We over-indexed in this area and I think it's been one of the biggest reasons for our success in the switch. Had we not done this, I don't think we would have been half as successful.

My advice to anyone in this position would be:

→ You need diversity.
→ It needs to be persona-driven

Roles to have in-house

Alice De Courcy · 1st

Group Chief Marketing Officer at Cognism - Technical SaaS revenue...

11mo · 🌐

How do you know when to hire and when to outsource in marketing?

In this post I am going to break down the structure of our marketing org:

Content Team:

This is divided into 3:

SEO pro's: they focus on executing our SEO plan, they are accountable to this and they hold targets in relation to this, which can be tied back to revenue

Content writing/journalist pro's: these are the people who are focused on writing editorial type content. They are tracking trends, they are acting and writing like journalists. There core focus is on key content engagement metrics, which again, can be tied back to revenue

Content distribution: this is the person who has been building our distribution approach and playbook, they have very clear metrics relating to key channels of distribution for us and again this can be tied back to revenue ultimately

Demand Gen Team:

This is split by segment: Enterprise | SMB | DACH

Enterprise: this team operates in a 'Pod', this means they are multidisciplinary and have a content team member sit-ing directly within their function

SMB: this team is running a fully demand first play. They hold 90% of the New Business revenue number for the whole company. Its a very diverse set of activities therefore that they execute that will be a mix of performant and brand actions.

DACH: this team again operates like a 'Pod' due to the nature of their marketing needing to be highly localised

Product Marketing Team:

This team is the cornerstone of everything we do in marketing. They have 5 pillars that they look after:

Market Intelligence

Positioning & Messaging

Product Launches

Sales Enablement

Information Flow

This team provides all the knowledge and information that is then taken and executed at scale by our customer and demand gen teams

Customer Marketing Team:

This team becomes more and more crucial as we scale. Again this is split into 4 key pillars of focus for their activities:

Advocacy

Expansion

Retention

Community

The customer marketing team also has a direct impact on revenue, through their work on expansion and their work on advocacy content that powers the demand gen engine.

Key roles that don't sit directly in marketing:

Marketing Operations:

This team sits within the wider operations team, but they are dotted line into marketing. This has really helped us to push the importance of understanding and building with marketing processes in mind organisation wide.

Marketing Development Reps (MDR's):

This team sits in Sales, alongside SDR's. They are responsible for dealing with all of the inbound demand that marketing creates. They are crucial to marketing's success. At Cognism this role has always worked best in the Sales organisation.

In my next post I will deep dive some of the pieces of the puzzle that we do outsource and how this has changed as we scale. Let me know if you would like me to expand on any specific points also.

#b2bmarketing #demandgeneration

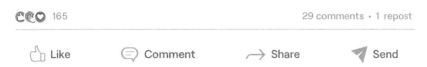

👍🙂❤️ 165   29 comments · 1 repost

👍 Like   💬 Comment   ➔ Share   ✈ Send

In an ideal world, you'd want all your skills and resources in-house. But sometimes that isn't realistic or workable and it also may not be what will deliver the best outcomes. I've outsourced certain skills many times. And I'll continue to utilise some external resources where it makes sense to do so.

However, in these cases, I'll explain why I wanted these roles to be within Cognism.

Content

Just to clarify, I think it's a great idea to use freelance writers to help scale the output of a content plan. Scaling with in-house headcount once you get to a certain stage, is not going to be the most efficient means of growing your output.

But one thing I think is important, is to have the foundations and expertise sitting in-house. And this is key because content is what drives a successful demand generation approach.

The way we do content at Cognism means there is a required in-depth knowledge and understanding of our personas' and of our product. There is also a requirement to work closely with our subject matter experts and to be close to all of the content output that happens in order to be able to best make decisions on how to curate and reproduce from this content.

Demand generation team

I don't believe you can do demand generation successfully, in the way we are trying to do it, without having an intimate knowledge of your target audience and of your product.

And fundamentally for this to work, we need to be tied to a revenue number, which someone external wouldn't be.

You need to be in your CRM. You need to be laser focused and obsessed with the activities and tactics that are bringing you revenue.

You need to be intimately connected to all parts of the marketing engine and wider business, from paid, to content, to sales.

A DG marketer needs to be deeply ingrained in the company, and this won't happen if they are external.

Product marketing

100% has to sit internally. There's no way of having this role sit anywhere else.

They're your expert on all things relating to your product. Your positioning. Your messaging. Market intelligence. The ins and outs of product launches.

Working between sales, marketing, product and customer success with all of the information flow that's required to make this role successful.

The hardest part of this role is managing the ever-evolving internal communication loops required to make it a success. There is no way this can be done unless the role is embedded in-house.

Customer marketing

Similarly to product marketing, this role is fundamentally required in-house. If you want to be customer-focused, then you need that resource to sit full-time in your organisation.

They need to understand your customers intimately or they won't be successful.

Marketing operations

This is an interesting one.

In the early days, the operations really sat with myself and our Global Head of Demand Generation as he and I were both very operationally driven.

We were comfortable working with our core marketing systems and more than happy to set them up. I think you need to be if you're an early-stage marketer.

It wasn't until two years into my Cognism journey that we looked to bring in a dedicated marketing operations role. Because operations were becoming such a time suck.

We had a demand generation team needing more systems, we had growing reporting needs, and ultimately, it was drawing time away from other critical tasks so there was a real need.

This role absolutely makes sense to have in-house, although they actually sit within our Revenue Operations team rather than marketing.

But having said that, we also work with an agency who have helped us to scale operationally to the next level.

I like the combination of an in-house expert coupled with an agency partner who has a wider knowledge base. The agency is working inside multiple MAP's and CRM's at any one time and they can pick and choose from the best of what they see and implement in order to advise on your organisation's requirements.

This has been a killer combination for us in taking our operational set-up to new heights. Top tip, choose your agency partner carefully. It is easy to be swayed by a senior agency employee, only to find your account handed off to a much less experienced person after signing up. I always want to know that the person who sells me on the partnership is also going to be the person doing the work.

Outsourcing

Alice De Courcy · 1st

Group Chief Marketing Officer at Cognism - Technical SaaS revenue...

10 mo · 🌐

What to keep in-house and what to outsource in marketing: part 2

Last time I looked at the structure of my in-house marketing organisation.

So here is my take on what you can outsource:

✓ Operations - we have found a killer combination here to be to work with a highly experienced Ops partner on an outsourced basis, but to accompany that with in house capacity, and this in house capacity should be an 'A player', experienced hire. This makes for a killer combination of experience and focus. This is our current combination and I only wish we did this a year ago.

✓Google Ads - now this is an interesting one. In the early days I moved this in house, I wanted to overcome the friction created by using an agency who were optimising for all the wrong metrics - those in platform, rather than in our CRM. My opinion now is that you can outsource this to a VERY good freelancer - shoutout MarketerHire for enabling this for us. We have actually seen a huge jump in performance by doing so.

✓ CMS/Web Dev - I think in the early days it is a luxury to have this in house, but it is vital to find a trusted partner and design an ongoing retainer with them to enable your team not to be blocked on any tasks requiring dev support. This could be an H2 2022 hire for me at our current rate of growth and team size.

✓ Innovation - sometimes you will need to inject innovation into your team and this can only be done by working with a partner/agency who is intensely familiar with your space and works/ed with numerous companies like yours. This will speed up your learnings, something that is critical if you are on a rapid growth path like we are.

Sometimes you will hit a stage of growth where hiring is not the most efficient option. It is not always the case that more people in the team = better results.

If you would like to learn more about how I approach things at Cognism, we are kicking off a series called 'Demandism' where we will be deep diving all things demand marketing and answering your questions live. First show coming this week, link in comments if you want to check it out.

👍❤️👏 86   9 comments

👍 Like   💬 Comment   ↗ Share   ✈ Send

When deciding which roles to outsource, there's one message that's important to keep in mind.

When might it be beneficial to have someone with expertise from multiple organisations? Meaning, when might this level of exposure from working with multiple orgs, help shortcut your internal learning period?

It's unlikely that an internal hire would be able to offer the same. Unless you can afford someone with ALL the years experience.

This combination really levelled up our set-up and maturity from a marketing operations standpoint.

One note though, I did this work. And I think that's important. When you work with outsourced talent they will need you to be able to think through all the implications as they won't have this experience and knowledge to draw on. I'm so in the detail that I can think about all the downstream impact of any changes and this is vital.

Web development is another great area to outsource.

When you find a good agency, stick with them. We have a monthly retainer with ours.

Recently, I was challenged by my CEO, asking why we should work with the same agency for the Kaspr projects we had after we acquired the brand earlier in the year.

He was determined we could find a French equivalent or another agency that would work just as well. I remember him saying, 'in all the world are you saying there is not a better or equivalent agency to yours?' Of course that is extreme, but it is also hard to argue against.

So I dutifully went ahead with a search for alternatives, but my warning was: we will go through a lot of pain to get there, and a lot of wasted cost. And I still believe the output will very likely not be as good.

So we chose another agency.

And very swiftly reverted back to our Cognism partner. They just weren't as good. Everything took longer, mistakes were made, and the end result was painful and not very well executed. So when you find a good one, keep them. They have come with me everywhere.

Outsourcing innovation.

I actually think this has been one of my biggest hacks to scaling learning and growth quickly. You could spend a year running various experiments and content processes trying to hit on the right way to do these things for scalable growth.

OR, you could cheat.

You could find those people doing it really well today, hire them on a project or consultancy basis and learn from them. Then instil those processes, skills and ideas into your team.

This is exactly what I have done at Cognism, and it has 100% enabled us to scale 10X faster than waiting to work it all out for ourselves.

Some of the people we have worked with to do this are:

→ **Refine Labs** - they were crucial in bringing structure to our paid social campaign set-up. They also gave us strong processes around reporting on our demand generation activity. Refine Labs are learning by working with multiple organisations every day. So their process of iterating and building out playbooks is much faster than ours would be.

→ **Gaetano DiNardi** - this is someone who has had huge success scaling multiple marketing organisations. He's the kind of talent we could never afford in-house, but provides us another cheat code to scaling our learnings much faster than we would without his advice and expertise. We don't need another pair of hands executing. Instead we need another strategic brain who can utilise their past experiences to advise during a stage of growth we haven't experienced.

→ **Todd Clauser** and **Obaid Durrani** - two people who truly get demand generation content creation. In a world of mediocre content, and very little-known process and structure around how to build a predictable high-quality content engine, Todd and Obaid are teaching us their methods. We have a transparent goal of upskilling ourselves to a point of redundancy for them. We actually utilised the budget for a DG content headcount to work with them. Why? We knew that we could hire someone in the role, and we could spend a year trying to build out a playbook for this function. Or we could work with people already doing it successfully today. People we couldn't normally afford to hire, and learn the playbook before we hire.

Catching a CMOs attention

 Alice De Courcy · 1st

Group Chief Marketing Officer at Cognism - Technical SaaS revenue...

11 mo · 🌐

How to write an outbound email that gets a CMO's attention...

1. Use Cognism to get my contact details

2. Be transparent about it and tell me

3. Personalisation, take the time to find a contextual hook that will actually form a meaningful relationship with me

Quality contact data + context = personalised outreach that gets attention.

Shoutout to Josh Levy and ON24 for this outreach.

#b2bmarketing #demandgeneration

Alice,

Used Cognism to get your details (you can't blame me for that one). Equally I don't even think you need us because you hit your target last year (130% of revenue target is CRAZY so well done).

But on the off chance, if you're open to exploring how driving deep purchase intent data direct into your CRM and MAP via engaging, always-on digital experiences could help you hit 140% this year, feel free to reach out and we'll

C👏❤️ 154   136 comments

👍 Like   💬 Comment   ➡️ Share   ✈️ Send

Shoutout to any SDRs wanting to do outreach to a CMO! Well, at least to me.

This example here is the best I've ever had from cold outreach.

I usually get about six or seven cold outreach LinkedIn messages a day. And maybe five or six emails too. And if I'm honest, I usually delete them right away. I can tell it's a pitch a mile off.

I do pick up cold calls, however. I mean c'mon, I sell mobile data – so I practise what I preach. But that doesn't mean I'll set up a meeting, or buy from you. I expect a good pitch.

Unfortunately, there's a lot of average prospecting out there. There's so much copy and paste. The bar really isn't that high.

Believe it or not, this is the only time I've had a message with this structure, even after posting about it to my LinkedIn. I literally told people how to outreach to me, but no one has ever replicated it.

But this is the only outbound message I've ever replied to. Ever forwarded to my team. Ever posted about. I booked in for a meeting after it as well.

It was just so refreshing to have someone be so open and transparent about what they were doing. Even better, they'd used Cognism to get my details (and my attention!)

And what topped it all off was the contextualised hook to show they had done their research and taken time to personalise the message.

This wouldn't have taken this SDR much longer than 10 minutes to do either. It could be very easily replicated.

Top tips:

1. Add value in your outreach. If you add value to me from the off, I'm going to pay attention. Or at least feel that I need to give you some value back. Treat your outbound like you do your email marketing, or a demand gen approach to social channels.

2. Call me. I answer calls. If I don't answer, leave me a voicemail. I always listen and I always remember the name of the company who called me.

Critical thinking

Alice De Courcy · 1st

Group Chief Marketing Officer at Cognism - Technical SaaS revenue...

10 mo · 🌐

Could you be harming your ability to generate greater demand by a philosophy bias?

Recently I was thinking about the movement from lead gen to demand gen, and how like everything, the best solution likely lies somewhere in the middle ground.

You will find some of the big demand gen proponents claim that you should always invest in brand over SEO, and that blog content is an outdated marketing tactic that belongs in the pre historic ages.

So here is my take, as someone who has made the switch from MQL's to a direct demand model, but who still believes in some of the more 'pre historic' marketing tactics such as SEO and blog content.

SEO: why would you not work to own the highest intent organic search positions for those terms most relevant to what you do and what you build your brand on? This in itself is a form of brand marketing.

The key is to make sure your content is truly valuable and not just written for the Google algorithm – but the two things are not mutually exclusive.

Blog content: demand gen philosophy is all about delivering valuable content to your audiences consistently. Now the problem with only delivering this 'in feed' on social channels, whether paid or organic, is that it makes repeat consumption of that content VERY hard. I have a slack channel full of LI post links for me to read later, but how much better would it be if there was one blog to refer to with all the same content, fully searchable?

For these reasons I am still going to double down on blog content and SEO, but the difference is, it's not for SEO algorithms or 'blog writing' sake. The content has to be valuable, it has to be subject matter expert led.

#demandgeneration

C❤️💡 85   12 comments

👍 Like   💬 Comment   → Share   ✈ Send

This post, for me, was all about the importance of being open to change.

Continuous learning is so important, because the environment you operate in is always changing.

I also think it's important not to get too comfortable relying solely on others to determine the right approach for you and your business.

You have to think critically and challenge the decisions you think aren't right just as much as the ones you think are.

This is a vital skill you need as a CMO.

Copying is easy. Knowing when to copy, what to evolve, and what to stick with is a little harder.

Listen and absorb, but still think for yourself.

That's why I don't feel protective about sharing my learnings with others. Because that's only half the story.

There's still an immense amount of work that needs to happen after taking on board lessons from others.

That's what will set you apart as a truly successful CMO and marketer.

Can you take what you learn, apply it to your business, and actually start executing it?

Making the switch from lead gen to demand gen

Alice De Courcy · 1st

Group Chief Marketing Officer at Cognism - Technical SaaS revenue...

10 mo · 🌐

Shifting from Lead Gen to Demand Gen - how to ACTUALLY do it

Phase 1: Things you can do right away that don't involve changing from an MQL model:

✅ Utilising a subject matter expert for your content

✅ Optimising the content you share on your linkedin organic channel - move from promotional to value led. See how we are doing this here: https://lnkd.in/efiZiRP4

✅ Upping your game on 'product'/ 'BOFU content' - ungated product tour snippets, CS video's running through use cases etc

✅ Build your own media machine and subscription channels: podcast, newsletter, youtube channel. Pick one and double down

✅ Changing the way you think about your blog: Not a place that content goes to die and is shared once on LI organic. It becomes the hub of searchable content for the media machine you are building. It is subject matter expert led, it is timely, it is journalistic and it is written by experts that are finding the trends from dark social

✅ Increasing the amount of video content you do

By doing all of this, you will actually set yourself up much better for success in phase 2.

Phase 2: Gradually weaning yourself off a reliance on the MQL model:

Step 1: Is how you should approach anything that you try that is 'new' and untested. It requires net new budget, a timeline and a hypothesis.

I requested a 5K/per month 'CMO testing budget', and I created a proposal that I would use this for 3 months to run the demand gen, ungated play on some of our top performing content, optimising for consumption and not for conversion. My hypothesis was that I would start to see an increase in inbound demo leads in line with this additional spend on demand gen.

We did. 47% increase, across the 3 months. This was trend and correlation, it was not specific at this stage, but it was enough.

Step 2: Split the funnel reporting

Understand the conversion rates from direct demo's vs MQL's.

Start reporting on this in exec meetings, start showing key stakeholders: rev ops, sales, CFO.

Then split out your MQL campaigns, don't look at them blended, understand your break even CPL on an MQL campaign:

Average deal size x Lead:CW = breakeven cost per lead

Then for any MQL campaigns that are under-performing on this, stop them, reallocate budget into demand gen activities and keep on only the top performing campaigns.

Soon your 'experimental' budget will double, without any material impact on your total MQL output. You have just consolidated and optimised.

We ran things like this for a further 3 months.

Then we had all the data we needed to start making a more dramatic shift.

#demandgeneration

C🌸🌿 330   41 comments · 6 reposts

👍 Like   💬 Comment   ↗ Share   ✈ Send

By this point in the diary you are aware that I have become a fully-fledged demand gen advocate.

But one of the questions I get asked most is always around how you practically make the switch.

My advice? Break it into manageable parts.

1. Things you can do right away that don't involve changing from an MQL model, such as:

→ Utilising a subject matter expert for your content.

→ Optimising the content you share on your LinkedIn organic channel. Move away from promotional to value-led content.

→ Upping your game on 'product', 'BOFU content'.

→ Building your own media machine and subscription channels. For example, podcasts, newsletters, and your YouTube channel. Pick what makes most sense for your audience.

→ Changing the way you think about your blog. It's not a place that content goes to die and is shared once on LI organic. It should become a hub of searchable content for the media machine you are building. It is subject matter expert-led, it's timely, it's journalistic and it's written by experts that are finding the trends from dark social.

→ Diversifying your content output formats.

By doing all of this, you will set yourself up for success in point two.

2. Changes that will alter the MQL model.

How we approached this:

We didn't go cold turkey, and I wouldn't recommend that you do either.

Step 1: requires a net new budget, a timeline and a hypothesis.

It's no different to how you should approach any new and untested activity.

I requested a 5k per month 'CMO testing budget', then created a proposal detailing how I'd use this budget for four months to run ungated, demand gen plays using our top performing content.

This involved optimising for consumption and not for conversions.

My hypothesis was that I would start to see an increase in inbound demo leads in line with this additional spend on demand gen.

Thankfully, I was right.

Over three months, we saw a 47% increase in these high-intent demo requests on our website.

Step 2: Split the funnel reporting

Funnel Averages					
Low intent		**High intent**		**Blended**	
avg acv	$1,509,00	avg acv	$1,678,38	avg acv	$1,637,92
lead:mb	7%	lead:mb	39%	lead:mb	13%
lead:ma	4%	lead:ma	34%	lead:ma	10%
mb:ma	63%	mb:ma	86%	mb:ma	76%
ma:sqo	46%	ma:sqo	59%	ma:sqo	54%
sqo:cw	12%	sqo:cw	20%	sqo:cw	17%
lead:cw	0.2%	lead:cw	4%	lead:cw	0,9%
lead:sqo	0.8%	lead:sqo	17%	lead:sqo	5%
leads for 1 deal	500	leads for 1 deal	25	leads for 1 deal	111

Understand the conversion rates from direct demos vs MQLs.

For us, we realised we needed 25 high-intent website demo requests for 1 deal, vs 500 MQLs from a content download for 1 deal. The ACV was generally lower on that content deal too.

Once you are tracking this data, you can start to report on it in executive meetings. Showing your results to key stakeholders like RevOps, VP Sales and the CFO.

Step 3: Take your reporting a step further

Split out your MQL campaigns, don't look at them blended.

Benchmark the performance against your break even CPL. This break even CPL is calculated by:

Average deal size X Lead: CW conversion rate

You'll likely be able to see some underperforming. If you do, then stop them. Reallocate that budget into demand gen activities instead and keep the top-performing campaigns on.

Soon your 'experimental' budget will nearly double without any material impact on your total MQL output. You have just consolidated and optimised.

We ran things like this for a further two months.

Then we had all the data we needed to start making a more dramatic shift.

Step 4: Change the split of our activities more dramatically. The split we went for was 90% demand gen and 10% MQL/lead gen. But you can slowly build towards this over time.

Your sales leaders aren't likely to push back on getting more time for their team to focus on outbound. It makes their performance easier to manage, makes them more accountable and gives them fewer excuses.

If you own a revenue goal, and you are saying to the CFO/CEO:

'I can still hit this goal with this change. I can fill the content deal gap with the increased inbounds that convert faster and at a much higher clip. I have got this.'

They can't really push back either.

Keep hitting this number, month after month and you earn the right to build this out further and further.

The best thing is that all the work you do in Step 1, fuels Step 2. And Step 1 requires no dramatic moves away from MQLs.

Shifting your reporting

The ugly truth here is that in the new demand generation world reporting gets a little bit murkier and complex. There's no single dashboard view or report that will be able to convey the full picture.

So where do you start?

Measure what you can attribute, but more importantly, measure what you can't.

It's good to be able to see what direct conversions your programs are generating, the more the better – always.

But, you don't want to use this as your north star. As it will inevitably lead you down the wrong path.

When I started out on my mission to transition into demand gen from lead gen I was satisfied if I was able to identify trends.

More create demand spend = increase in our overall volume of direct, high intent demo requests.

Ensure you are set up to track your direct attribution by having strict UTM formatting in place. Also enabling self reported attribution on either your thank you page post demo or on the demo form itself.

This hybrid attribution framework will give you key insights into what parts of your create demand activity are having the greatest impact.

When it comes to measuring the success of our create demand activities, the focus shifts away from leads towards reach and engagement.

You want to answer the following questions. 'How much of my audience am I penetrating?' This measures reach. And, 'how well received is this content?' This measures reach.

Examples of metrics that matter here are:

→ Impressions, reach, video views, frequency.
→ CTR, engagement rate, likes, comments.
→ Qualitative feedback/shares.
→ Traffic, time on page, bounce rate.

When looking at these metrics, it's important to run three comparisons to help inform effectiveness.

1. Performance over time.

2. Performance against benchmarks.

3. Performance against existing programs.

Note: you will need to build out your own benchmarks for your organisation. It's also important to measure programs against the right metrics.

For example, it may be tempting to measure all ads against CTR as it's easy. But, if your objective is reach or video views, you'll be measuring against the wrong objective. Below is good overview of how to group key metrics and report back against them:

Scale	Spend
	Reach
	Impressions
	Clicks
	Frequency
Ad Engagement	CTR
	Clicks/User
	Net Engagement Rate
Video In-Feed Consumption	Thumbstop Ratio
	50% Views/User
Distribution Cost	CPC
	CPM
	CPR
Website Engagement	Pages/Session
	Bounce Rate
	Avg. Session Duration
Conversions	Goal Conversions (Analytics)
	Cost/Conversion
	Conversions (Platform)
	View Though Conversions
	Assisted Conversions
Pipeline (Salesforce)	Salesforce Leads
	SQOs/Pipeline
	Revenue

As a CMO it is also critical you have a handle on your top line numbers that matter:

→ Marketing revenue generated ($)
→ Number of deals
→ SQO pipeline amount
→ High-intent leads (demo request on website)
→ Total paid spend to acquire these
→ Blended CAC
→ ACV
→ CAC Payback Period

Your conversion rates across every stage of the funnel are also critically important. Any drop in any one of these could signify an opportunity for improvement and optimisation.

For example, I saw a decline in our direct demo to SQO conversion rate.

A look under the hood revealed that we had hit our MDR capacity. We were routing too many leads to our reps, meaning they couldn't spend as much time per lead.

We now have a clear model and inflection point for the number of leads per MDR and our optimal conversion rate expected from this.

It's not 2010 anymore

Alice De Courcy · 1st

Group Chief Marketing Officer at Cognism - Technical SaaS revenue...

9 mo · 🌐

Top 3 reasons why marketers no longer need to collect MQL's?

1. The software and technology now exists that you can just get access to a tool/database like Cognism which will mean you have unlimited access to contacts in your ICP - and the best part? Their details are actually correct. No false data input. AND their details are maintained - no data decay issues.

2. MQL's from content downloads that no-one reads is just the same as a cold contact from a database like the above, the conversion rate difference will be very minimal and the cost per contact and quality is far higher if you utilise such a tool vs expensive LinkedIn lead gen campaigns.

3. Intent data now exists to give us insights into when someone is actually in market, enabling you to refine the contacts you pull from such a tool and actually start to increase your conversion rates. A prospect that is surging on a high intent keyword is far more likely to convert than just a random content download contact. And imagine if you had the mobile number of such a contact and 98% accuracy on all their contact details?

I talk a lot about the move from lead gen to demand gen, but the key for unlocking this for me in many ways was actually having a tool like Cognism to fill the MQL gap and actually increase conversion rates.

#demandgeneration

👍❤️🎉 128   10 comments · 2 reposts

👍 Like   💬 Comment   ↗ Share   ✈ Send

Marketing today is not the same as marketing in 2010.

I think this is a very important part of the lead gen to demand gen shift discussion.

We're all told it's what we should be doing, but very rarely is it framed in these terms.
Technology and tools now exist that mean we don't need to run e-books or gated forms to collect contact data.

We can actually use these tools to generate much higher quality, validated contact data, in an 'always on' fashion. Often at a fraction of the cost.

The best bit?

The intent is no different from an e-book download and a contact you get from one of these contact data providers.

We know because we've tested it.

Stop and think about how you consume content.

If you actually did download an e-book on a topic that interests you - which, let's be real, a lot of us don't bother to even download now, do you actually read it?

Or does it sit on your desktop. Collecting dust and taking up precious RAM space!

Even if you did read some of the content, there is absolutely nothing to suggest that you are looking for the company's solution or tool as a result.

So what's the great news?

There are tools that can actually help you identify contacts that are in the market today, intent data providers.

Using intent data + contact data, you now have some level of 'real intent' insights on which to run some outbound plays that might convert at a profitable rate.

And the even greater news?

This means that it's no longer marketing's job to provide sales reps with contact data in order to keep them dialling.

Marketing can now focus on the job of bringing in actual high-intent, declared demand through the website.

On-demand, ungated, free content

Alice De Courcy · 1st
Group Chief Marketing Officer at Cognism - Technical SaaS revenue...
8 mo · 🌐

〽️ Netflix subscriptions are down but on-demand, un-gated, free content is the way forward for B2B marketing.

Here are 3 ways we are thinking about this at Cognism:

1️⃣ On demand nurtures - we are just launching our first one of these and excited to see the results. If you enrol a contact in a nurture sequence and expect them to open, read and engage with your emails in a linear fashion then you need to think about how you consume content. Do you ever think – 'Oh wow I'm in this crazy personalised email nurture that is serving me up the perfect content exactly when I need it'. The reality is we don't know where the buyer is sitting in their search or awareness and we need to allow them to consume the content when and in whatever order they require it.

2️⃣ On demand, continuous events - just starting to put my thoughts and ideas together on this one. Why do we wait all year for 'the industry event' of the year, where the speakers and content have been planned months out and may no longer be relevant, or we turn up to the event just to be disappointed in the quality of the content? What if we had continuous on-demand talk tracks running across the year featuring relevant speakers of the moment?

3️⃣ Paid social promotion of your best content, always on, to your ICP, no forms, just content and value

If marketers spent more time thinking about how to make the most valuable content and then most importantly, make that content as easy to consume as possible, on demand, then they would unlock true B2B marketing success.

The truth is that this stuff is hard to do and figure out, there is no playbook for it yet, no one has figured it out, so you need to be willing to ideate and set the path, rather than follow a well trodden, broken one.

#b2bmarketing #demandmarketing

👍❤️😮 145   20 comments

👍 Like   💬 Comment   ➤ Share   ✈ Send

Forget the funnel. Forget all you've learned in B2B marketing school. And forget anything you've heard from big analysts and tech firms.

Once you can leave this mindset behind, you unlock the keys to starting to truly stack growth.

The old way of building an email nurture:

→ Map out the buying funnel.
→ Serve content across a timed series of emails that cover each stage of the buying funnel.
→ Expect that you will convert at the end of the nurture because you have taken the buyer across each funnel stage.

Top tip: no one opens an email and thinks, 'yes great, I am in the MOFU stage and this content really aligns to that. I'll keep my eye open for my BOFU email in one week, when I am certain I'll be ready to buy!'

Instead, there's a new way to do things:

→ Send sequenced emails, but aligned with reality.

Most people will miss the majority of the emails in the sequence. Or only one email actually piques their interest that day to engage and click.

So every email should be a delivery mechanism for an 'always on' resource that can be consumed by the reader whenever it suits them.

You want to give your audience the freedom to decide which content they consume.

Okay, so now what about campaigns?

These used to be gated content initiatives, usually containing an e-book that ran for six weeks, after months of planning.

Why?

Because that is how we had been taught to do marketing. You don't see jobs for 'always on marketers', you see jobs for 'campaign marketers'.

But what if you served your best content all the time? Ungated, friction-free. What if it could be activated across several channels, adapted and refreshed as frequently as the data dictated?

Who is to say that during the six weeks you run your 'campaign', that your prospect is going to be in the market?

It's much better not to leave this up to chance, trying to catch them at the right time.

Instead, add value continually, so the moment they move themselves in the market (yep, they move themselves), you are front of mind.

The final one I included in my post was the idea of 'always on' events.

I haven't seen this done yet in B2B and it's still on my radar as something I would like to try out at Cognism. One for the next book and for 2023!

Imposter syndrome

 Alice De Courcy · 1st
Group Chief Marketing Officer at Cognism – Technical SaaS revenue...
8 mo · 🌐   •••

3 years ago I joined Cognism as Head of Marketing.

We were a team of 3 Marketers.

We were under $3M in revenue.

There was no predictable monthly revenue or even targets for Marketing.

Fast forward and today we are a marketing team of 20.

We have scaled revenue to well over $25M.

And Marketing is consistently contributing to over 55% of that number month over month.

Sometimes its good to stop, reflect on where you have come from, and celebrate a little.

I think the thing about this I want to be honest about is that I actually didn't think I could do the role.

I turned it down originally primarily because I was scared to fail.

I am now 100% a believer in the best things you will achieve come from being uncomfortable and pushing yourself.

And there is NO way this would all have happened without the amazing team we have been growing.

Looking forward to looking back again in another 3 years!

#b2bmarketing #demandgeneration

 1,541   124 comments

 Like   Comment   Share   Send

This was my first 'viral' post!

It is crazy to look back sometimes, thinking about how much has changed. How we have managed to scale and the speed at which we have grown.

I mentioned in the post that I didn't think I could do this job before I took it on. And believe it or not, that imposter syndrome still lives in me today. I have to fight daily to have the confidence to make the decisions I need to in my role.

Since I wrote this post, we have surpassed 40M, with over 100% growth this year. And an important point to note is that marketing has predictably driven the majority of this new business revenue month over month. Contributing well over 50%.

But I still doubt myself.

And every day I will have a decision to make where I feel uncomfortable.

The biggest difference from three years ago to now? I'm starting to trust myself more and more. I embrace being uncomfortable. I actually thrive on it now.

I get excited by new challenges. No two days are the same.

Rebranding Cognism

Alice De Courcy · 1st

Group Chief Marketing Officer at Cognism – Technical SaaS revenue...

1mo · 🌐

We can finally share what we've been working on...

Same Cognism, just more us!

Rebrands are often a bit of a taboo in marketing.

It can be seen as 'busy work' not necessary work that will actually move the dial on what really matters, revenue.

So why did a revenue focused CMO go to the board and CEO and request to rebrand...

It wasn't because I didn't like our logo, it wasn't because I wanted to be seen to make an impact, it was because we were being slowed down by our old brand and that would ultimately start to impact our ability to hit revenue numbers.

We were reinventing the wheel at every stage, we were in 'brand limbo'.

I will deep dive this and more in the latest Demandism live which you can sign up to in the comments. Lots of mistakes and lessons I can share to help you make your next rebrand a smooth one!

#demandgeneration #b2bmarketing

🌀💬❤️ 263   41 comments · 8 repost

👍 Like   💬 Comment   ↪ Share   ✈ Send

It took me three years before I decided to rebrand Cognism. I'm a firm believer in if it ain't broke, don't fix it.

But it was broken. We were in a state of brand limbo.

Everything we did meant re-inventing the wheel. There was a lot of precious time and resources wasted and we were being slowed down a lot!

So I decided to push for a rebrand, but underneath the project scope was a whole lot more, it was about:

→ **Defining our messaging, mission and positioning.** More importantly, getting all the executives to align around one vision.

→ **Re-writing all the copy on our website.** Introducing new pages and removing redundant ones.

→ **Re-creating website experiences and journeys.** We had moved to a fully un-gated model, but our website still required work to reflect this.

→ **Consolidating our operational set-up from a forms and landing pages perspective.** We went from 400+ forms down to 20.

→ **Migrating our CMS code base to a truly scalable, self-serve drag and drop solution.**

When thinking about doing a rebrand, you have to fully scope the project.

It will touch so many elements and you need to ensure that you can maximise the outcome. To do this, your planning has to include as many of those critical items as possible.

One thing I'd recommend is keeping a laser focus on output during the process.

I kept my team very sheltered from distractions until the very end. I didn't want any loss of output or any 'we'll wait until the rebrand' rhetoric.

It's precisely those things that give these types of projects such a bad rep.

In hindsight, I may have kept them too sheltered. I say that because when the time came for the final push, which required a big team lift, there was some initial push back.

I could have avoided that if I was more transparent during the process.

But I felt determined that we couldn't stop delivering. Nothing ever got blocked by the rebrand. As far as the company was concerned, one day the website was purple with lines, and the next it wasn't!

We also built a mini brand hub. This enabled our organisation to easily access all the newly branded assets on the morning of the switch.

Tools like Seismic and Mailtastic enabled us to centrally manage and update our email signatures and collateral. So the lift on individuals was minimal and it as easy as possible to rollout. A huge win for a seamless transition!

How to structure your content team in a demand gen org

Alice De Courcy · 1st

Group Chief Marketing Officer at Cognism – Technical SaaS revenue...

7 mo · 🌐

How to structure your content team in a demand generation first strategy:

When we made the shift from lead gen to demand gen, a lot of things changed.

Content was no exception. We are now all about maximising engagement, about building a media machine, about acting like journalists.

This meant the way we structured and went about producing our content needed to change as well.

Repurposing content that was written for SEO purposes – focused on matching the intent of our target search terms, was not going to cut it anymore.

eBooks were no more.

So we split our content team into 2.

We have one part of the team who are our 'always on' media content machine. They are spending time in the places our customers consume content, they are searching out stories and they are producing content in all formats based on this.

This spans content with our subject matter expert, our newsletters, our organic company page, our blog and other content resources such as templates and video's that we see trending.

Then we have our SEO team, they are solely focused on writing intent first content that will drive meaningful traffic from Google. A mixture of both capture and create demand depending on the keywords.

The great thing is that the content we produce from our media machine, truly helps us set our SEO content apart. We don't 'write for Google', we write for people, we write for intent first. And we differentiate our content by being experts on topics we choose to go after.

And the third content structure is something we will be rolling out in H2, with a content person sitting in each of our Demand Gen Pods, focused on ensuring our 4 DG content buckets are always full of the best content possible within each pod: thought leadership, product, content and social proof.

#demandgeneration #b2bmarketing #content

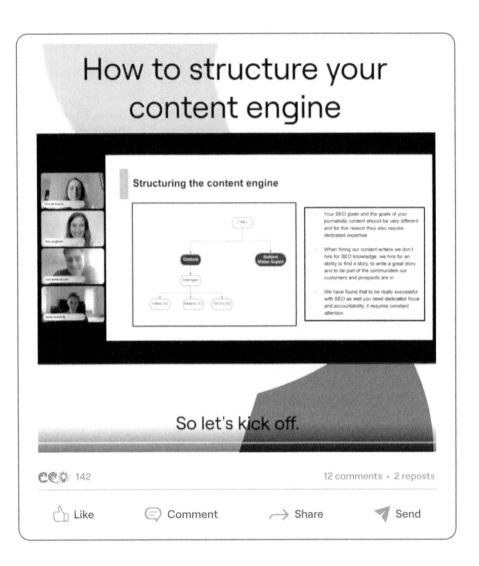

We have three different content roles within the Cognism marketing team structure.

This setup is to maximise our media machine aiming to both capture and create demand with our content.

We've built a brand around our content differential, something I have already spoken a lot about throughout this diary. This was my vision for it on day one.

I knew our advantage was being lean, being able to act quickly and to ship lots of output.

Our processes have evolved with our move from lead generation to demand generation, and with the separation of activities across create demand and capture demand.

These changes meant needing to rethink the content roles we had in the organisation. And to look at how we structured ourselves in order to achieve success.

Content Function 1: SEO

Our SEO efforts are focused on capturing demand. This team spends its time working where the commercial intent is greatest.

There is so much continual effort that goes into obtaining, maintaining and expanding your SEO footprint that it has to be separate from your other content functions and roles.

The skillset, the focus and the type of content required are very different to any other parts of the content engine.

Content Function 2: Journalistic Content

Early on in my shift into demand generation, I doubled down on the idea of building a media machine. I felt like a critical part of this was a change in the way we produced and went about writing our content.

Old way: map out the blog content titles we wanted to cover a quarter in advance.

We used ad hoc feedback, and ideas from the demand gen team and the sales organisation to generate these titles. As well as desk based research.

New way: commit to a base level of content delivery per week/per month, but don't commit to titles.

Have a place for storing title ideas for times when inspiration is low. But otherwise, act like a journalist. Go out and find interesting people and stories to cover that are relevant today. Make connections with subject matter experts and get really good at interviewing them.

This requires a big shift in mindset and also in the profile of the type of person you hire into the role.

Content Function 3: Demand Gen Content

These people sit within the demand gen org. They know their persona intimately and are tasked with content in all of its formats. That means video, scripts, blogs, webinars, podcasts, snippets and more.

They are the 'create demand experts'.

Their content is powering all the create demand activity the demand generation team executes.

This is without a doubt the hardest role to hire for.

So many people assume when they see 'content' in a role, that means they'll be writing blogs or other long-form content only.

They only know how to operate based on a pre-planned calendar and they aren't comfortable building out processes that will power a create demand content powerhouse.

These people need to be agile. They need to be content creators with a flair for creativity and a strong bias for action and delivery.

You want someone in this role who is able to help ideate on key content themes. They need to take those themes, and map out the best content format for the core deliverables. They've also got to understand how they will take one asset and multiply that into many.

This is a unique and new skillset. It is arguably probably better-suited to a DG marketer that would like to focus more on content, than it is a traditional content marketer.

Don't backslide

Don't retreat to Google Ads.

When times get harder and budgets come under greater scrutiny, it is hard for marketers to justify continuing to invest in create demand tactics.

But the simple truth is that Google Ads is only going to get MORE expensive, there is less volume and more bidding.

And if you halt your create demand investments now, you are going to be slowing growth for when the climate changes. And it will change.

Instead optimise your Google Ads campaigns to focus on maximum efficiency – not based on in platform metrics, but based on revenue.

This will leave you with budget, even if only small, and it is this money that you should be using to continue to create demand.

The good news is that while most people will run back to Google Ads, the cost of create demand paid advertising reduces and you can find your underpriced attention.

It's not all or nothing and finding the right balance is the key.

#demandgeneration

194   30 comments · 1 repost

Like   Comment   Share   Send

Having operated in a pandemic and now a looming recession, I do feel I can speak from a point of experience here.

There's no doubt that budgets will be tightened, and you'll be tasked to do more with less.

But this shouldn't mean retreating back to purely capture demand activities.

At Cognism our general rule regarding budget split is 30% demand capture and 70% demand creation.

As budgets are squeezed, we'll maintain this ratio.

Typically when you first get started running a create demand play, you'll need to wait 2X your sales cycle length to start to see the benefits in terms of pipeline and revenue.

The compounding impact of its continued execution is how you really start to stack growth.

Retreating back to Google Ads and capture demand only activities will make life incredibly difficult when you get asked to do more again.

It'll also make life much harder while you operate in an already difficult economic environment.

So my advice would be to hold your nerve.

Maintain your splits, but optimise. Optimise for CRM metrics and revenue. Reduce down any capture demand campaign that is not delivering in your CRM.

This will give you money back to continue to invest in creating demand.

I'd also use this time as an opportunity to focus on activities that are time heavy, not $ heavy.

How good are you at creating content in all of its formats?

Have you built a repeatable process around a live content event and the post content production afterwards?

Are you maximising every content opportunity for the greatest output and gain?

Have you spent time on your website and landing page experiences?

Could you be creating better self-discovery journeys?
Is there room to improve your key funnel conversion metrics like demo:MA rate?

Could you launch a direct to AE routing experiment to increase this?

Audit all the possible areas of focus that don't involve more $, but require more time.

Map them out in relation to effort versus impact. Then start to work through them one item at a time.

You didn't always have the budget you have today, and you were still successful.

Chances are you have more resources in other ways available today. So make these work for you.

Attracting talent

 Alice De Courcy · 1st
Group Chief Marketing Officer at Cognism – Technical SaaS revenue...
6mo · 🌐   · · ·

There is a movement happening.

The last few months we have been hiring into the marketing team at Cognism (and still are!) and what we have been seeing is that there is movement happening, it's still relatively small in the UK right now, but we are riding the wave and benefiting hugely from it.

What do I mean?

There are a few unicorn marketers who have been following Chris Walker and Refine Labs content for some time now. In some cases some of these marketers are implementing the demand gen first approach directly into their organisations.

Some are still trying to get internal buy-in, but they are not defeated and fundamentality they buy into this shift in b2b marketing, and importantly they understand it.

At Cognism we have been very open about our journey from lead gen to demand gen and Chris and I have documented this pretty openly across a number of podcasts over the years. Starting with back in the day when I would firmly defend the place of an eBook within a marketing strategy. We've come a long way!

And this transparent journey and discussion has meant that when we open up roles in the team, we are attracting these unicorn marketers.

Yes we massively reduce the number of applications we get for these roles with statements like :

'Refine Labs, State of Demand Gen will be one of your top listened to podcasts',

But I would much rather have 5 great fit profiles, than comb through 100 'demand gen' marketing profiles who's experience is firmly still based on traditional lead gen plays and who have no understanding of the concept of creating demand and why it is important.

There is a movement and I'm incredibly excited by the quality of talent it is surfacing and that we've been lucky enough to hire a lot of it! H2 is going to be exciting! If you want to hear from some of this amazing talent, we have another Demandism live to sign up for - link in comments.

 247   25 comments

---

👍 Like   💬 Comment   ➡ Share   ✈ Send

I feel incredibly passionate about this one.

I've already mentioned that hiring should be a CMOs superpower.

Building a following of marketers as a result of our shift from lead gen to demand gen, has been one of the biggest wins for my team.

Thanks to our openness about the journey, they regularly read and engage with our content. Another perk? They also want to work for us!

It proves that Cognism is an innovative place to work, and it's somewhere that prioritises marketing investment.

It's a successful example of marketing being a revenue-generating engine.

It's a marketing team where you know you will be setting the standard for what good B2B marketing looks like and there's no following well trodden paths. It's all about creating our own 'new way'.

We have managed to build a community that breeds like-minded marketers who buy into our philosophy, who are forward-thinking and comfortable operating in the unknown.

I've never had an easier year of hiring.

The quality of the inbound talent that has been applying to positions has been incredible, with personalised cover letters like the one from diary entry no.50 becoming the norm.

There's a movement happening and I am incredibly proud that Cognism is building a home for these unicorn B2B marketers.

The 10% more mindset

Alice De Courcy · 1st

Group Chief Marketing Officer at Cognism - Technical SaaS revenue...

4 mo · 🌐

The 10% mindset.

A lot of people ask me how I got to a position of being CMO and I've thought a lot about this as a result.

The single biggest driver I would attribute it to is the idea of a 10% more mindset.

So what does that mean?

It's the idea that anyone can always do/give 10% more. This extra 10% means that you don't have to be the brightest person in the room, you don't even need to be the best at marketing, but you will be the one who works the hardest at getting there.

This 10% mindset does not work if you only do it in short bursts.

It has to be a consistent approach to work or something in your life that you practice every single day and for every single task.

It's probably not going to be the most popular approach to getting to a CMO role, because it is surprisingly hard to follow through with, but when I look back at what really made the difference, it was this.

The compounding impact of practicing a 10% mindset.

#b2bmarketing #demandgeneration

 238   30 comments · 2 reposts

 Like   Comment   Share   Send

Don't underestimate the compounding effect of going above and beyond what is expected, asked for, or required.

I believe the key to the 10% more mindset is that it's sustainable. It doesn't result in burnout, or short bursts of over-productivity, followed by an inevitable dip.

It's had a huge amount to do with any success I've had throughout my career and earlier life. I've always striven to be the hardest working person, even if I can't be the brightest.

It comes back to what is in your control. You can control how much effort and time you put into something. You can control the consistent execution.

Applying this basic principle can have huge benefits over time.

If I could summarise the type of CMO I am in three words they would be:

→ Action-driven.
→ Obedient.
→ Hardworking.

They may not be the most exciting, but it means I am reliable.

I'm consistent, and I have a 10% edge over many others as a result. And importantly, this 10% manifests in action. This can be enough to put you ahead of your peers and to land you that CMO job.

My predictions

Alice De Courcy · 1st

Group Chief Marketing Officer at Cognism – Technical SaaS revenue...

3 mo · 🌐

Today content marketing has to be much more than writing blog posts and whitepapers.

If you are executing a create demand approach to marketing, pivotal to its success is grasping the requirement for your content to diversify well beyond blogs and whitepapers.

A content marketer operating in this create demand world needs to be able to take content in one format and reskin and repurpose it into many many others.

They should be able to listen to a webinar or live event, spot audience engagement on key topics/points of interest and take that and use it to inform their strategy for producing 3-4 short form video's, organic LinkedIn posts, create demand paid social ads and maybe a blog post.

They must be able to deep dive the success of all the formats of content they are producing, getting comfortable finding dark social insights, and feeding that back into the content creation process.

At Cognism we have these new breed content marketers sitting in our demand gen pods.

Why?

I believe they need to be close to all the content that is being produced and distributed within their target persona, every ad, webinar, blog posts, live event, newsletter. They need to be intimately knowledgeable about that persona, and ultimately, they need to be fully comfortable producing content that may more traditionally have been seen as a function of the demand role than a traditional content role.

#demandgeneration #b2bmarketing

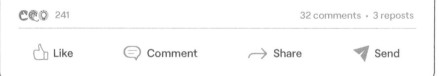

😊👏👍 241   32 comments · 3 reposts

👍 Like   💬 Comment   ➔ Share   ✈ Send

I'm going to put it down in writing.

I predict content marketing will experience a big shift over the coming years.

There will be a departure from what has been traditionally expected of the role...

The old way required you to be a good writer that can conduct desk research. You had to be able to produce multiple articles (of varying lengths and formats), with some SEO optimisations.

The new way will need writers to understand their audience deeply. They need to be able to interview and collaborate with subject matter experts to give their work authority. They need to be as confident briefing a storyboard for a video as they are writing an interactive pillar page.

This new breed of content marketer understands the requirement for different content types and formats. They are across all the content they produce and brief for their audience. And they're capable of building scalable and repeatable processes. Enabling their content engine to scale.

They operate like journalists, producers, content curators and top-class interviewers.

Finding this type of content profile in B2B marketing today is very hard. If you are a content marketer or a demand gen marketer that would like to specialise in content and can adopt this approach, you're going to be in high demand!

My dream demand gen marketer

 Alice De Courcy · 1st
Group Chief Marketing Officer at Cognism – Technical SaaS revenue...
2 mo · 🌐   ● ● ●

Amateur actress or CMO?

Following on from yesterday's post, here is an unedited insight into how I spent my day on Tuesday. We ran a filming day, where we got all of our subject matter experts scheduled to film a whole batch of campaign and always on content.

What went into this day?

- Script/outline creation and writing
- Film scheduling
- Talent briefing and booking
- Content audit and planning of our campaigns and always on
- Planning out the post production prioritisation and editing process

Sounds so much more fun and less boring than building another gated ebook landing page and ops flow while blowing up your laptop refreshing zaps that have broken 'just because'!

It's clear from this unedited video I am not a natural behind the camera, but it's a great new challenge and a welcome change in requirements from my role that have happened because we have we have made the switch to demand generation.

Thank you to our amazing videographer Emily Liu and Demand Gen Manager/Producer Jamie Skeels

👍❤️😊 234   48 comments

 Like   Comment   Share   Send

I was recently talking to a peer about the demand gen role in marketing and what skills were required to be good at it. I started reeling off a whole list and I suddenly realised how different this was to the profiles I would have traditionally looked at.

My dream demand generation marketer is completely bought into the mindset of balancing creating demand with capturing demand. They understand that the buying journey is not linear and that buyers move themselves in-market.

If they get this, then it's likely they understand how to create content for their audience. And importantly the mechanisms for delivering that content. Always on, all the time, to everyone.

They would hopefully have a portfolio of work to showcase how they do this, and in that work there would be absolutely no e-books or whitepapers!

They would be confident in managing 'the talent', producing videos with them, enabling interviews and building repeatable processes around these initiatives to stack growth.

Much like the changing content role, demand generation looks very different today, and the talent pool that can execute on this is small but growing. Most of them work for Cognism!

Conclusion

Phew, and we've made it to the end.

If you've read through each of my diary entries – thank you. I know that was a lot of information! Hopefully you found it interesting and have been able to learn from my experiences.

I'd love to know which of the entries resonated with you the most, which you found useful. Or what you'd have done differently if you'd been in my position.

Connect with me on LinkedIn and send me a message.

And if not, then maybe I'll see you again in a few years for round two, Diary of a CMO: The Remix.

Printed in Great Britain
by Amazon

18908709R00113